Cynicism
and the
Evolution
of the
American Dream

Cynicism
and the
Evolution
of the
American Dream

Wilber W. Caldwell

Potomac Books, Inc.

Washington, D.C.

HN
90
.P8
C35
2006

Library of Congress Cataloging-in-Publication Data

Caldwell, Wilber W.
  Cynicism and the evolution of the American dream / Wilber W. Caldwell.
    p. cm.
  Includes bibliographical references and index.
  ISBN 1-57488-985-0 (hardcover : alk. paper)
  1. Public opinion—United States. 2. Social psychology—United States. 3. Cynicism—United States. I. Title.
HN90.P8C35 2006
303.3'80973—dc22

                                                                    2006003626

Printed in the United States of America on acid-free paper that meets the American National Standards Institute Z39-48 Standard.

Potomac Books, Inc.
22841 Quicksilver Drive
Dulles, Virginia 20166

First Edition

10 9 8 7 6 5 4 3 2 1

Contents

Contents

Contents

Preface

> Dream other dreams, and better. Strange,
> indeed, that you should not have sus-
> pected that your universe and its contents
> were only dreams, visions, fiction!
> Strange because they are so frankly and
> inherently insane. . . .
>
> Mark Twain, *The Mysterious Stranger*

The American Dream has evolved slowly. It began with an optimistic individualism that exuded both an idealistic hunger for liberty and a materialistic thirst for property. The story of the ongoing struggle between the idealistic side and the materialistic side of the American Dream chronicles the history of our nation. It is the saga of the persistent forces of liberty and democracy and their labors to withstand the gales of America's reckless, preemptive, acquisitive appetites. With the watchdogs of the American Dream of liberty nipping at its heels, the American Dream of property has stumbled through a series of increasingly materialistic and often disappointing landscapes, until today, for many, it has finally come to manifest little more than a faint, shallow, selfish, unfocused longing for celebrity and easy money. For a disturbing number of young Americans today, the American Dream is simply to win the lottery. It is the theme of this book that the disturbing growth of cynicism in America today is the result of a recent shift in the American Dream.

Like all national dreams, the American Dream has mirrored our national experience and our collective character as well as reflected our national mood, which has run a parallel course all the way from idealism through realism and skepticism to cynicism. Idealism is fostered by hope. Realism is fostered by experience. Skepticism is fostered by uncertainty. And cynicism is fostered by disappointment. And so it comes full circle, for at the root of all disappointments lie the trampled remains of hope.

Of course, the slow corruption of the American Dream and the corresponding deterioration of the national mood did not scribe a linear descent. Like all human histories, it has been more like an erratic pendulum, swinging in arrhythmic oscillations both great and small. In the broadest of overviews, the American experience can be summed up in three distinct epics: first, the colonial period, dominated by "the old philosophy brought to the new world from the compact societies of Europe, with its doctrine of determinism and its mood of pessimism;" second, the buoyantly hopeful romantic era beginning around 1800 and "influenced by French romantic thought and a spirit of robust individualism;" and third, beginning just after the American Civil War, a period characterized by widespread materialism and "the slow decay of romantic optimism."[1] In the twentieth century the continued gradual buckling of the nation's romantic ideals and aspirations under increasingly complex, modern weights has effected a widespread loss of faith in the national dream and wrought the many bitter disappointments that lie at the root of a diffuse sense of ambivalence and an unfettered cynicism that infect America today.

But the broadest overview often risks oversimplification, and if we look more closely, we can see that each of these three American eras is characterized by its own internal pendulum swings, each scribing a shorter national journey from hope to despair. Obvious examples might be the materialistic exuberance of the 1920s followed by the utter disillusionment of the Great Depression; the youthful hopefulness of the 1960s followed by so many heartbreaking assassinations; or Lyndon Johnson's dreams for a "Great Society" that were all too quickly overshadowed by a desperate national preoccupation with the Vietnam War. The list goes on and on. Certainly the Great Depression was not the first national economic disaster. There was a devastating financial crisis in 1837 and again in 1892, for example. Nor were JFK, RFK, and MLK our first martyred national heroes. And certainly Vietnam was neither the first nor the last American military entanglement to utterly disillusion the nation.

Like the heavenly bodies in Copernicus's errant and impossibly complex model of the universe, these pendulums are in constant motion, pendulums attached to pendulums. There are even those today who suggest that, as the pendulums swing in ever smaller arcs, the maddening rapid-fire frequency of the current oscillations from optimism to pessimism has become, in and of itself, a source of cynicism.

Accelerated swings from expectation to disappointment have affected not only our political and financial outlook. They have also insidiously molded our attitudes regarding almost every aspect of our lives: work, religion, family, class, race, ethics, art, crime, nature, humor, and so on. Indeed, they continue to shape our very worldview and self-image as well as to color our perceptions of our culture and society. What is worrisome is this: as the twenty-first century begins, further corruption of the American Dream seems to have spawned an unflinching, self-perpetuating strain of cynicism that is blind to these cycles and thus neither tempered, diminished, nor reversed by periods of good news or by the prospect of better times. In short, today many Americans remain cynical no matter what.

Thus, today we are facing America's most terrifying

enemy ever: an indigenous, insurgent army made up of millions of our own citizens. We snipe at ourselves from behind impregnable barricades of cynicism, mocking efforts to move ahead, scoffing at once-cherished national ideals. Diverse and resourceful warriors, we wield our cynicism as both sword and shield. We are resolute in our cause, for after a hopeful beginning, we have experienced a lifetime of disillusion and disappointment. "We have met the enemy, and they are us."[2]

What is the nature of such cynicism? What are its historical roots? What are its present causes? How does it manifest itself today? How does it relate to the American Dream, and what are its effects on modern American life? Perhaps most importantly, how are we to oppose such an insidious and unyielding aggressor? In these questions lie the subjects of this book.

America still has the potential to remain a great democracy, but she faces a grave crisis. There is serious work to be done, and as citizens, we must take our stewardship seriously. If we fail to do so—if we succumb to cynicism's numbing venom— we are lost.

Acknowledgments

My sincere thanks go to my friend Bill Chaloupka both for what he wrote and for what he did not write. I was fascinated by many aspects of Bill's book, *Everybody Knows* (University of Minnesota Press, 1999), an insightful study of cynicism in American politics. This fascination led me well beyond politics. I was inspired to expand on Bill's work, and to explore the historical roots of cynicism in America and its effect in the broader spectrum of American life and culture.

Most important, I wish to express my loving gratitude to Mary Fitzhugh Parra for devotion, tea, and sympathy, and for her super-human patience in the face of my endless ponderings.

Part I:
Cynicism and the American Dream

1

The Face of the American Cynic

As the events of twenty-first century begin to unfold, the epidemic spread of cynicism in America continues to mushroom unchecked and little understood. Most Americans are vaguely conscious of, and strangely fascinated by, their own cynicism. At the same time, most are unaware of the peril it represents to our democracy, our ideals, our institutions, and our way of life.

The flamboyant cynicism of H. L. Mencken and the aging Mark Twain is gone. The American cynic is no longer a witty, worldly critic. He has barricaded himself in private redoubts of unremitting mistrust. Alone, disappointed and bitter, he is most often melancholy and withdrawn. Gone are the clever sarcasm, the poignant irony, the knowing wink, and self-assured sneer. Today's cynic has no energy for such endearing humor. Only rarely does he allow himself the satisfaction of a mocking aside, a knowing nod, or a theatrical wince of pain. Modern American cynics are hard to spot, and thus, today, cynicism in America is more widespread and diffuse than most Americans are given to imagine. Cynicism in America has many hidden faces.

Profiles in Cynicism

The following profiles present composite characters created for the purpose of illustration, not real individuals.

Glen H. Most people who know Glen H. feel that he has lived something of a charmed life. He grew up in an upper-middle-class suburban neighborhood near Chicago in a time of plenty. A gifted athlete and a mediocre student, Glen attended Indiana University on a football scholarship and graduated in 1976. Born in 1955, he was too young to be involved in the Vietnam war or in the youth movements of the late '60s and early '70s. He was athletic, affluent, educated, and good-looking, the all-American boy, a late-arriving member of the baby boom generation, the largest, most self-assured, generation America has ever produced, with the largest sense of entitlement. Through his childhood and youth, Glen was certain that his lot in life would surpass that of his prosperous parents, and that his children's lives would be better yet. He was equally sure that his college diploma was a magical key to the doors of success, his personal guarantee to the riches of the American Dream. After college Glen went to work for a large construction company as an estimator. He married in 1980, and soon he was the father of two girls. Today Glen lives with his wife and two teenage daughters in a very nice neighborhood in Evanston, Illinois, where he works for the city as a building inspector. Most would say he is still living the American Dream.

But dreams are not always what they seem to be. They are will-o'-the-wisps, fraught with illusion and uncertainty. After a few years, the contractor for whom Glen was an estimator went bankrupt. Glen sought other work, but the job market was flooded with his fellow baby boomers. The jobs he did find all turned out to be to dead ends. With loans from his father and father-in-law, he started a small construction company of his own in 1985. This proved to be a disaster. The jobs he over-bid, he did not get; the jobs he under-bid resulted in losses. It was not long before his little company failed. In the resulting financial upheaval, he lost his house. After a few more false starts, he ended up in Evanston with his present job and a fat, new mortgage. The pay is poor, but at least he has a few fringe benefits. To make ends meet, his wife works, and the girls have college loans and part-time jobs.

What happened to that rosy future the baby boomers had once envisioned, that prosperous future everyone had taken for granted? Today Glen sees himself as a man somehow helplessly fixed in time, unable to move either forward or back. He feels vaguely disappointed and betrayed. Slowly, he withdraws. He hates his work, and he has no outside interests. It never occurs to him that his job has a noble side, that he is a public servant, charged with protecting citizens from fraud at the hands of building contractors. Indeed, he knows contractors (and all businessmen, for that matter) to be untrustworthy. In fact, he feels that most people are just out for themselves. He is also convinced that government has its own manipulative agenda apart from the public it pretends to serve; he is certain that most public officials are not concerned with the problems of the average citizen. This kind of diffuse, reflexive, ingrained mistrust is the hallmark of cynicism. Glen has a lovely, healthy family, a nice home in the suburbs, two cars, and all of the material things a man could desire, and yet he feels himself to be a failure. His future seems uncertain: he believes in nothing, and he is cynical about almost everything.

It is not that Glen H. has failed to achieve a good life. It is that his life failed to meet his expectations. His dreams were never in line with reality. They did not allow for partial success.

Caroline R. and Roger T.
Caroline R. and Roger T. are brother and sister. They were born to well-to-do parents in Charlotte, North Carolina, in the mid-1940s. They both attended private day schools and fine liberal arts colleges. Today Caroline and her husband operate their own small business, which Caroline inherited from her father. Her brother, Roger, is retired after a very successful career in the printing business. Caroline has become an extreme conservative, while

Roger never veered from the uncompromising liberalism of his youth in the '60s. Despite their widely divergent political, economic, and social views, they are both American cynics for virtually the same reason.

If pressed on the issue of what is wrong in America today, Caroline will confess that she feels that it is a problem of too many "rights." She believes in individualism and the work ethic, and she is angered by government programs that artificially interfere with the free market system and the mechanisms of competition and commerce. She feels weighted down in her business by governmental interference: tax forms, employment forms, social security reports, equal opportunity requirements, safety regulations, unemployment claims and the like. "I am from the government, and I'm here to help you," she likes to sarcastically quip.

On the other hand Roger feels that American rights are in danger of being eroded by government, and that the programs now in place to protect these rights are too few, poorly conceived, inefficiently run, and sadly ineffective. For those who claim to be "politically liberal, but fiscally conservative," Roger will reply, "That means you know what is right, but you just don't want to pay for it." Both siblings are deeply disappointed in government, Caroline because, despite Reagan, government has been unable to shrink itself and return the nation to *laissez faire*, and Roger because, despite Clinton, government has failed to reinvent itself and produce a modern, streamlined, responsive body that looks after the common good of the nation.

Despite the polarity of their views, today both Roger and Caroline see government as a shadowy, inscrutable monolith that seeks its own interests while cynically voicing platitudes about the interests of the people— a great faceless, totalitarian monster that is well beyond the control of anyone. Despite their heart-felt political opinions, they both feel politically powerless and perceive this powerlessness to be universal in contemporary American politics. Parties and candidates flaunt platforms that appear to offer a choice, and yet, when the smoke of the empty battles of rhetoric clears, there remains only a dull sameness. Although the siblings attach very different meanings to the words, both believe in the American Dream of liberty and democracy and in the freedom to rise. Motivated by this belief, both vote regularly, even though both are secretly sure, with the blind knowledge given only to the indefatigable cynic, that their dreams, like their votes, are meaningless, just so much dust in the wind.

Helen A. Helen A. is 37. She is divorced, lives alone, and teaches high school in Boston. Helen is a woman of regular habits. Each evening she prepares her supper and then watches the evening news while she eats. It sometimes seems to her that the news never really changes, that she is stuck in some sort of time warp in which she is destined to endlessly repeat each day without variation of any kind. She tries to concentrate on the news. Here are soldiers with a fallen comrade, here the birth of quintuplets, here a horrific auto crash, here a politician, here a weather map. The words and images seem to blur; they come and go so fast that she cannot properly ponder their meaning; they begin to run together. Helen is unable to attach orderly meaning to them. Which demand her attention, action, concern, or pity? Which are trivial, superfluous, weightless? At first, she sees the world in sharp contrasts of black and white, but eventually everything blends into a uniform, monochromatic gray. Because she is unable to clearly distinguish good from evil or the meaningful from the mundane, she is unable to recognize any of the subtle variations in between. For Helen all is equivalence.

Helen A. suffers from an insidiously widespread form of cynicism that I call the "cynicism of the matter of fact." It is the product of the lightening pace of the modern world. The media, especially television, spread it most effectively, but it is not only television news that feeds Helen's cynicism. It is the preponderance of the assaults on her senses, sheer informational saturation. When one attempts to inform one's self in all directions at the same time, a judgmental shutdown is bound to ensue. Eventually, like Helen, one perceives only equivalence. The inevitable result is cynical indifference.

Mark G.

Mark G. was a Dodgers fan. He grew up in Fresno, and his boyhood heroes were Sandy Koufax and Don Drysdale. As he grew older, he began to fully appreciate baseball. It was no longer just a game. It was a metaphor, it stood for something, and the men who played it were not just men, they were heroes, symbols not just for athletic excellence, but for excellence in general, for competitive spirit, for fair play and for the dignity of human kind. That's what heroes are about—they are larger than life models for how to live. Or so Mark came to believe.

Somehow all that changed. Mark doesn't get out to the park much anymore, and when he does it makes him kind of sad, but not the bittersweet sadness of nostalgia. It is the sadness of something missing. There are no more heroes. The players are better than ever, yet they seem somehow small and petty. They don't play the game for itself anymore, or even for winning or loosing. They play for the money. Or so it seems to Mark.

Then they had the audacity to strike. That was the last straw. The loss of his heroes constituted a great disappointment for Mark, and he has since become cynical about baseball. Today, these feelings are reinforced by charges of the widespread use of steroids and other performance enhancing drugs by so many of the game's elite. Not only do the heroes of the modern diamond appear to have forgotten the true meaning of baseball, many apparently cheat not so much to win as to satisfy financial ambitions.

At the bottom of it all, Mark's cynicism is not really about baseball at all. Baseball is a metaphor for life. Nobody else seems to give a damn anymore—why should he?

Eliot R. Eliot R. is 22. He lives in rural Kansas and works part-time for a friend who is trying to start a pressure washing business. Raised by well-educated parents in suburban Kansas City, he was never given to books. Eliot managed, after a great deal of effort, to earn a degree from a small community college. After this daunting experience, Eliot wants nothing having to do with reading, writing, mathematical calculations, or paperwork of any kind. He deeply rejects anything academic, bureaucratic, theoretical, or clerical. He loves the out-of-doors, and his dream is to be a rancher, but he knows that agriculture today is successful only on the massive scale achieved by the big agribusiness co-ops. He understands that, except for the hobbyist operations of gentleman farmers, the small farm in America is no longer a viable proposition. Eliot thought about growing herbs commercially or starting a small organic farm, but he soon found all of this took land and labor and capital.

Eliot is as stranger in his own land, adrift in a society not of his own making. Because he is not from the country, he is subtly rejected by the rural population whom he admires. Because of his opinions and his carefully cultivated "redneck" manners, he is rejected by the urban population to which he belongs. He feels frightened, alone, uncertain, and disappointed. In a nation once filled with small farms, his highly individualistic agrarian dream of the land is sadly out-of-date. An American cynic at a very young age, Eliot fears, mistrusts, and cynically mocks the modern world, while romantically longing for a world that no longer exists. For a variety a reasons, many of the nation's young people are similarly adrift, today.

Cynicism and Irony

According to young Jedediah Purdy in *For Common Things*, a recent plea for social participation in America, many of the nation's youth feel helpless and disenchanted. Purdy informs us that young people are convinced that "the direction of history" is beyond their control, and there is a widespread feeling "that the drift of things is inevitable." *For Common Things* contends that Americans today, especially young Americans, are afflicted by what Purdy calls "ironic skepticism," a condition characterized by a "wry detachment that avoids taking anything or anybody seriously." "The ironic individual," Purdy tells us, "practices a style of speech and behavior that avoids all appearance of naiveté—of naïve devotion, belief, or hope." At the core of such "irony" lies the fear that the appearance of sincerity may open the ironist up to betrayal, disappointment, or humiliation; he thus mistrusts his own speech. To protect himself he employs his irony to "drain words of evocation, beauty and moral weight." In so doing, the young ironist avoids honestly facing the world around him, and through his irony he remains "unmoved by . . . neighbors, the world" and himself.[1]

For some curious reason Purdy, like many of today's observers of detached irony, seems unwilling to face the fact that what he describes as "ironic behavior," is really nothing more than a manifestation of a common defense of the cynic. Not all cynics lash out with cynicism's critically clever sword. Some are withdrawn, employing their cynicism as a shield. Clearly Purdy's ironist is such a one. Purdy's own words confirm the ironist's underlying and motivating cynicism. "We are wary of hope, because we see little that can support it." Later on he writes, "Somewhere along the line we came to believe that everyone's motivations are in some measure selfish, ignoble or neurotic." This is the very definition of cynicism.[2]

Purdy's ironist has a cynical view of politics, which is "presumed to be the realm of dishonest speech and bad motives. Moreover, it is presumed that everyone sees through the speech, that the motives are as transparent as the new clothes of the emperor." Later he writes, "To talk about politics today is to presume insincerity. It is the first requirement of even modest political sophistication to understand that public figures neither say what they mean nor mean what they say."[3]

From all of this it is clear that Purdy's "skeptical ironist" is really nothing more than a card-carrying modern American cynic, albeit of a somewhat self-conscious sort. What is more, he may be the ultimate cynic, for not only has he come to mistrust the world around him, he has also come to mistrust himself. As Purdy puts it, "He disavows his own words." Purdy's ironist struggles in the "disappointed aftermath of a politics that aspired to change the human predicament in elemental ways, but whose hopes have dissolved into heavy disillusionment."[4] Call it what you will, this is cynicism.

True ironic detachment is much more subtle in its assessment of the current state of affairs. Accordingly, it can be elusive and difficult to define. It is far a more forgiving way of looking at things, a multifaceted, often uncertain, view of the postmodern world that acknowledges the simultaneous validity of many, often contradictory interpretations of reality. Irony arises from ambiguity. It may simultaneously entertain the possibilities of outcomes of both hope and disappointment. Cynicism mocks the prospect of any hopeful outcome. Accordingly, it is highly resistant to all of the usual remedies, undaunted by calls for improved values or more belief.

Jedediah Purdy, like many observers of detached irony, holds out at least some possibility for trust and hope, because in the end his solutions for our national malaise are found in abstract arguments for "responsibility," "attentiveness," "work," and "dignity," and in renewed participation and faith in public life. All of this will presumably somehow be accomplished through individual conversion and persuasion. Perhaps the ironist can be converted or persuaded. The cynic cannot.

A Cynical Nation

The faces of the American cynic are many. Cynical politicians disingenuously mouth slogans of liberty and national security in order to manipulate the uncertain masses. After repeatedly witnessing such manipulations, the rank and file slowly withdraw into the cynicism of perceived powerlessness. Cynical business leaders fraudulently manipulate world communications and energy markets while manufacturers attempt to harness the shifting fads and fetishes of popular culture in order to hawk overpriced merchandise, thus further fueling the fires of cynicism that burn deep within the fabric of our nation. The utter transparency of both political and commercial advertising only serves to make matters worse.

The reasons for cynicism in America today are as varied as the faces of the American cynic. Certainly and to some significant extent, we might at first conclude that such cynicism is justified. But the price of such a conclusion is astronomically high, for once cynicism reaches its reflexive stage, the stage at which cynical reactions become automatic and unthinking, we not only lose the power to act, we lose the power to reason. Advanced cynicism is blind. It is difficult to refute, because it eschews all reason. Worst of all, it is sedentary, unable to act except for an occasional mocking critique of tradition or innovation. All solutions are rejected as naive. The result is gridlock. Cynicism clings to the *status quo*. It denies all possibility of moving either forward or back. By definition, if the cynic offers up any active solution at all, he ceases to be a cynic.

How do we combat such an enemy? First, we must arm ourselves with a workable definition of modern cynicism. We must then critically evaluate our enemy. When, if ever, is cynicism appropriate? What are its strengths and weaknesses? Next, we must consider our national dreams, for cynicism, we will find, is the product of disappointment, of dashed dreams and abused faith. In order to fully understand the evolution of American cynicism, it will then be helpful to review our national history, focusing on our dreams, their successes and especially their failures, along with the resulting cynicism. Lastly, in light of all our discoveries, we must closely examine American cynicism in our own time, its causes and effects. Only then will we be able to put a clear face on cynicism in America. Only then will we attempt to propose a battle plan designed to defeat the insurgent enemy who destroys from within.

2

Toward a Definition of Cynicism

> The power of accurate observation is often called cynicism by those who have not got it.
>
> George Bernard Shaw

> I am not at all cynical, I am only experienced—that's pretty much the same thing.
>
> Oscar Wilde

There is a great deal of talk about cynicism these days. But how many have stopped to consider what the word really means? If pressed on the issue, most Americans would probably shrug their shoulders and confess that, in one way or another, down deep, they perceive themselves to be card-carrying cynics. But how many understand cynicism's subtle complexities and far-reaching implications?

Cynics have been around since classical times. In ancient Greek and Roman times the affront of classical cynicism was hard to overlook. Classical definitions and examples are quite clear and easy to read. But cynicism has evolved. As the present era unfolds, cynicism is still mutating. Its meanings now embrace broad new undercurrents. It is today becoming something more veiled, more insidious, more enervating; something often described as a disease: "infecting," "spreading," "contaminating."[1] Today, the force of cynicism threatens to undermine our society, and most of us are still unsure what the word really means. We often mistake it for skepticism, for irony, for critical realism, for pessimism, or for misanthropy or use it where simpler words will do. Meanwhile, the term is being tossed about so carelessly that it may soon cease to have meaning at all.

Socrates Gone Mad

According to *The Oxford English Dictionary, Second Edition*, a Cynic was, "one of a sect of philosophers in ancient Greece, founded by Antisthenes, a pupil of Socrates, who were marked by an ostentatious contempt for ease, wealth, and the enjoyments of life; the most famous was Diogenes, a pupil of Antisthenes, who carried the principles of the sect to extreme aestheticism." Except for the connection to Antisthenes, which many modern scholars have abandoned,[2] this antiseptic definition is technically correct. But what it doesn't tell us about early Cynicism is everything!

The roots of the term "cynicism" go back to Diogenes, the paradigmatic Cynic and one wild character, indeed. According to Peter Sloterdijk, "The appearance of Diogenes marks the most dramatic moment in the process of truth of early European philosophy." Sloterdijk describes the "great split" begun by Diogenes. On one hand there was "grand philisophical theory," argued by Plato and by a long and impressive list of Western philosophers right on down to modern times. On the other hand were Diogenes and his subsequent followers, "a satirical-literary troupe of skirmishers," who "pantomimically and grotesquely carried practical embodiment to an extreme." Diogenes smelled the "swindle of idealistic abstractions," and to oppose such swindles, he created a "tradition of satirical resistance and uncivil enlightenment," a kind of mock philosophical theater of the street.[3]

In their study of the legacy of classical Cynicism, R. Bracht Branham and Marie-Odile Goulet-Caze call Cynicism "the most original and influential branch of Socratic tradition." But the Cynicism of Diogenes and the early Greek Cynics was not exactly a philosophy. It did not put forward a "systematic ensemble of beliefs." Rather it was something more akin to a "way of life," a moral practice "capable of guiding the individual toward happiness, simplicity, freedom and autonomy." For Greek Cynics, high-minded philosophy "offended the truth"; while nature provided an observable moral model. Since society did not conform to nature's form, its values were considered false. Thus, "rather than arguing by careful and precise dialectic, which is the true Socratic method, Diogenes intervened with . . . living example." He railed against the great philosophers of the period with shocking criticism and shameless pantomime designed to scandalize polite society. In short, Diogenes and the early Greek Cynics "distrusted words and demanded action."[4]

Given their objection to the formal rhetoric of philosophy, it is not surprising that we have almost nothing in the way of written contemporary evidence concerning the early Cynics. What we do have is a seemingly bottomless deposit of anecdotes describing the outrages of Diogenes and his followers. This lack of documentation may be a problem for historians, but it should not be a problem for philosophers, for just how much of the oral tradition is actually true does not really matter. What matters is the beginnings of a tradition of satire, parody, diatribe, and criticism by outrage—not just Diogenes with his lamp or living in his tub, but Diogenes publicly picking his nose, farting, pissing, and even masturbating before Plato, Socrates, and the rest. Plato is said to have called him "Socrates gone mad." His crude exhortations urged a "return to an original simplicity and to a state of nature," and they constituted a deliberate public "rejection of shame: the cornerstone of Greek morality." Here was, and still is, an argument that "respectable thinking does not know how to deal with." Some of these stories may be embellished and some may not be true at all. No matter. As William Chaloupka reminds us, "That is the point." What is important is that the "crudities" of Diogenes, "so resonated with the audience that they kept adding lines, creating stories and reinventing him."[5]

The word "cynic," is generally thought to come from the Greek, *kyon,* for dog. It is said that the term came into use because Diogenes and his followers lived in public like dogs, in order to demonstrate their radical idea of freedom by using "any place for any purpose." Some contend that the Cynics found the appellation so appropriate that they defiantly claimed it as a metaphor for their novel philosophical stance."[6] Other sources link the "doglike" qualities of the early Cynics to dog-like shamelessness and to the dog-like ability to distinguish friends from enemies. This last is especially apt owing to a dog's proclivity to drive enemies away by barking at them.[7]

The Beginnings of Modern Cynicism

The Cynical movement lasted for almost a millennium in antiquity. In Roman times it became something of a "mass movement," and the sight of Cynics begging and preaching in the streets was common, especially in the East. With the end of the classical period, Cynicism disappeared for a time, only to re-emerge in the Renaissance as a powerful ideological force and as a robust literary tradition in satire and parody aimed at "defacing the false values of the dominant culture." Cynicism was a critical tool for writers and thinkers like Erasmus, Montaigne, Thomas More, Rabelais, Ben Johnson, Jonathan Swift, Rousseau, Diderot, and Nietzsche.[8]

With the success of such luminary apostles, Cynicism began to penetrate deep into the roots of modern Western consciousness. But as the modern era approached, what evolved was not exactly the same Cynicism that Diogenes had practiced. By the middle of the sixteenth century cynicism simply meant biting criticism, and the term "cynic" was defined simply as "a fault-finder." Later the definition began to expand, embracing cynical technique characterized by "wordplay, biting sarcasm, and merciless witticism." By the beginning of the eighteenth century, we see the modern definition begin to emerge. Modern cynicism implied something shrewder and more personally embittered than mere faultfinding, something more acidic, more mocking — something that wielded a slashing sword "against the arrogance and moral trade secrets of higher civilization." Finally in the middle of the nineteenth century we find this definition: "Cynic: A person disposed to rail or find fault. Now usually one who shows a disposition to disbelieve in the sincere goodness of human motives and actions, and is wont to express this by sneers, and sarcasm. . . ."[9]

The last definition articulates the core of what has become the "standard" modern definition of cynicism, the element of deep mistrust in human motives coupled with a bold satirical reaction or with sneering sarcasm. *The New Oxford American Dictionary* defines "cynical" as "believing that people are motivated purely by self-interest, distrusting human sincerity or integrity." *The American Heritage Dictionary* calls a cynic "a person who believes that people are motivated by selfishness," and then more generally, "a person whose outlook is scornfully and often habitually negative." And *Webster's Third New International Dictionary of the English Language* informs us that "cynical" means "1. given to faultfinding, sneering and sarcasm. 2. given to or affecting disbelief in commonly accepted values and in man's sincerity of motive or necessitude of conduct: accepting selfishness as the governing factor in human conduct. 3. exhibiting feelings ranging from distrustful doubt to contemptuous, mocking disbelief."

Although mistrust and sarcasm are important elements in any modern definition, when taken alone, they offer only a simplistically one-dimensional picture of modern cynicism. Even when modern dictionaries throw in secondary definitions like, "concerned only with one's own interests and typically disregarding accepted or appropriate standards in order to achieve them," or "pessimistic, as from world-weariness," or "doubtful as to whether something will happen or is worthwhile," [10] we are still left only partially informed in our efforts to define modern cynicism's true nature and scope. Where are the trampled expectations; the embittered, rapier wit; the impregnable defenses; the shattered unrealistic ideals; the detached hopelessness; the ironic smile; the mock, stoic melancholy; the sarcastic little wince of pain, and the detached withdrawal that lie behind the modern cynic's wily smirk? All of this and more must be included, or at least implied, in a comprehensive modern definition of cynicism.

In order to arrive at such a definition, we must break things down a bit. When we consider the definitions of other writers, thinkers, and pundits who have contributed to the literature of modern cynicism, we find a surprisingly diverse array of descriptions of current usages of the term. Many begin with something basic like the definition detailed above, and then supply details by discussing different "types" or "modes" of modern cynicism. Others include definitions that describe cynical "techniques" or behavior. Still others rely on definitions that try to explain the true nature of cynicism by exploring its causes and/or effects in order to imply its true nature. Most provocative of all are those who describe cynicism as a kind of mass survival strategy arising out of, and employed to deflect, the bleakness of the modern human condition. All of these are serviceable approaches, providing useful insights. But only when taken together do they begin to form a useful, if not concise, description of what it means to be a cynic.

Cynics and Kynics

As we have seen, by the time the modern era began, cynicism had come to mean something quite different from the ancient

Greek Cynics' call for a return to the simplicity of nature and their scandalous modes of criticism aimed at high-minded philosophy. However, despite the changing face of modern cynicism, there still exists today a tradition akin to that of the early Cynics. To distinguish the antics of the classical Cynic from the despair of the modern cynic, the practice arose of capitalizing references to the lingering remnants of the "Cynicism" that originated in ancient Greece, with its bold forms of criticism, and using the lower case to refer to modern cynicism characterized by manipulations and mistrust. This is not without its problems, because the behavior of the modern Cynic is a bit different from the antics of the ancient Cynic. A better solution is that proposed by Peter Sloterdijk in his definitive work, *The Critique of Cynical Reason*. To describe the modern practice of overt criticism and protest Sloterdijk uses the term *kynicism,* from the Greek *kynismos*, thus relating it to, but also distinguishing it from, ancient Cynicism and thus reserving the term "cynicism" to describe the domain of the mainstream modern cynic.

According to Sloterdijk, modern kynicism begins with individualism and can be distinguished from its darker brother, cynicism, in that it is "pantomimic, wily and quick-witted" and "has its existence in resistance, in laughter, in the appeal to the whole of nature and a full life." Kynicism is the type of cynicism that Nietzsche describes as "a different approach to saying the truth." Certain aspects of the modern hippie movement supply excellent examples of modern kynicism. And recent pop culture is filled with kynics: Hunter S. Thompson, Randy Newman, and Elvis Costello to name but a few. Many contemporary comedians are kynics; indeed, laughter is a primary weapon of kynicism, and according to Sloterdijk, jokes are a key element. Al Franken, Richard Pryor, and Robin Williams are good examples. In the humor of the kynic, "vices and insults, ironies and mockeries have their largest playing field." Thus, the term *kynicism* provides a useful way of setting the boisterous, active, focused antics of the modern kynic apart from the malicious espionage of the modern cynic.[11]

Powerful Cynics and Powerless Cynics

At this point, if we set the slapstick world of modern kynicism aside, and refocus on our definition of modern cynicism, we can now point out two distinct branches, including "both a way of life for the powerful and a way for citizens to live, understand the world and express themselves."[12]

The "standard definition" of a cynic, one who mistrusts the motives of others, points to a widespread loss of faith. This is the "citizen cynicism" of the powerless masses. Loss of faith, disappointment, disillusionment—all are common currency in the psychological economy of the "Modern Condition" (discussed in detail in chapter 8). As its disappointing transactions are repeated over and over, numbness sets in, and the cynic begins to exhibit "contempt for whatever might be proposed." Having learned from experience, this new cynic "refuses cheap optimism. New values? No, thanks. With the passing of hope, self-interest pervades, and a detached negativity comes through that scarcely allows itself any hope, at most a little irony and pity." As William Chaloupka observes, this diffuse brand of cynicism "resists and subverts the important social themes, such as faith, rationality, utopia, and reform. It undermines how we think about important concepts: freedom, authority, self, change, and stability." Sloterdijk quips that the citizen cynicism of the powerless "is the widespread way in which people see to it that they are not taken for suckers."[13]

Everybody knows the wisdom of the old adage, "Power tends to corrupt; absolute power corrupts absolutely." But few know the next line of that familiar quote, "All great men are bad men." The powerless cynic will smirk and nod knowingly at this, for he is convinced that the powerful remain powerful only through "cynical" lies and manipulations. The cynicism of the powerful is characterized by "overt deception and rhetoric that exceeds what can realistically be accomplished."[14] Such rhetorical manipulations usually include the exploitation of cherished ideals including democracy, liberty, and the American Dream. Sloterdijk describes "refinement in the knowledge of domination" as a process by which those in power "sacrifice the hearts of the subjugated." This process includes lies that the powerful do not themselves believe, but that they let others believe.[15]

In the end, it all becomes circular, in what Jeffery Goldfarb calls "legitimization through disbelief." "Leaders use rhetoric which neither they nor their constituents believe, but which both leaders and followers nonetheless use to justify their actions." For example, the proclamation of "the American Dream accomplished" may be employed to both cover up and to ignore a wide range of American nightmares. With this kind of rhetoric flying about, "pieties about the values of democracy" soon appear quite empty. In the face of such hypocritical transparencies broadcast from above, the powerless cynic recognizes the sham of the powerful as they ascend the ladders of power; in this recognition his feelings of disappointment and powerlessness increase; he is thereby reinforced in his cynicism, and his cynical prophesies become self-fulfilling. "If we believe that all in authority justify their actions through elaborate rationalizations of privilege, then the principles upon which authoritative actions are . . . based will disappear," thus further freeing the powerful to engage in cynical manipulations. This is just one of many situations that produce loops of cynicism. As we shall see, there are many more, for modern cynicism has many faces.[16]

Thus, we see a self-renewing cycle involving two distinct types of modern cynicism—the cynicism of the masses, who mistrust those in power, and the cynicism of the powerful, who shamelessly attempt to deceive and manipulate the masses. At the heart of each type lies a fundamental mistrust in human nature. The citizen cynic is convinced that those in power are abusing their power, and the powerful cynic is convinced that the masses are not intelligent enough to recognize his abuse or not brave or resourceful enough to stop it.

Routine Cynicism

Although we call it by a single name, cynicism today wears many costumes. It may appear in myriad disguises from the baggy, clown-like vestment of the angry jester to the somber mourning suit of the melancholy, the withdrawn, or the disillusioned. In fact, the varieties of cynicism are so diverse that they cannot easily be arranged according to a logical hierarchy of sets and subsets. As William Chaloupka is quick to point out, cynicism may even be "more than one thing." This is what makes a good definition of it so elusive. In *Everybody Knows,* Chaloupka deals primarily with political cynicism, and describes a world in which cynicism has split into varieties that differ significantly from one another. "Cynics compose themselves differently in different roles," he informs us, and "there are specific characteristics and implications for . . . various particular roles." To further confuse the issue, the different types of cynicism often work as an "ensemble," but as Chaloupka warns, they do not always interact in predictable ways. For example "the cynicism of leaders does not [always] simply produce or reflect the cynicism of citizens,"[17] as in the example above.

Perhaps the form of cynicism most frequently referred to in recent literature on cynicism is something referred to as "routine cynicism," "unthinking cynicism," or "perpetual cynicism." Cynicism of this sort occurs automatically after repeated disappointments. The cynic has seen it all before. So many proposals, solutions, and ideas have been put forth, have been tried and have failed; so many promises have proved to be nothing but hollow rhetoric; so many programs have betrayed so many of the grand ideologies upon which they were purportedly based. Eventually one reacts cynically to virtually everything. Why discuss it? Why believe again only to see one's resurrected ideals re-crucified? Why even consider it? It won't work. Nothing ever works. Here the cynical response is automatic, routine, unthinking, and thus, here is a cynicism that is immune to even the most compelling of logical arguments.

"Routine cynicism" has been defined as "an automatic response before one studies the situation, . . . a philosophical loss of trust in the . . . possibility of goodness. . . ." This is a most dangerous form of cynicism because as a "philosophical" axiom, it is invoked at the most primitive level. Neither logic nor reason nor evidence nor popular opinion will have its say. Arnett and Arneson call this "existential mistrust." In *Dialogic Civility in a Cynical Age* they describe it as a "blindness that leads us to fail to recognize the actions of a friend, a genuine crisis, or ideas that demand our attention and response. Life is too often lived with the conviction that something or someone has already gone wrong or will go awry." Of course, cynicism has its place, and it is often useful and appropriate in cases where the rhetoric is "consistently at odds with the action." The problem with routine cynicism is that it touches everything and ignores those people who do speak in a manner that is consistent with their actions. In short, the routine cynic has lost the ability to choose when to be cynical. His cynicism is automatic, and thus, he has lost the ability to address any ambiguity. He misses all the subtle shades of gray that exist between good and evil. Many scholars suggest that routine cynicism in its most extreme form finds its origins in an (accurate) "appraisal of our modern social condition" and the contemporary moral vacuum in which we exist.[18]

In *The Cynical Society,* Jeffery Goldfarb discusses what he calls "perpetual cynicism," which "dominates the assumptions of our political and cultural life." Like routine cynicism, perpetual cynicism occurs "without much reflection," so that "not only do we not recognize the cynicism; we confuse it with democratic deliberation and political wisdom." Perpetual cynicism is a product of conflicts inherent in the workings of democracy. According to Goldfarb, it is "produced and reproduced in democracies because the necessary balancing act between the private interests and the common good provokes suspicions and differences in judgment. People suspect that actions in the name of the public good actually serve individual private interests." Goldfarb also discusses what he calls "mocking cynicism" — a kind of "knee-jerk" resignation that mocks efforts to live a moral life as naïve. The result is helpless indifference and an odd kind of support for the status quo. According to Goldfarb, when the powerful employ false pretense to accumulate more power the powerless observe this and "their sense of powerlessness increases, and when despite this sense they try to act according to moral principles . . . mocking cynicism ridicules their efforts."[19]

In *Heirs of the Dog,* Daniel Kinney also recognizes a kind of "unthinking cynicism" when he observes that the cynic "displays general contempt for ideals of all stripes." Likewise, William Chaloupka points to a similar type of routine cynicism that foregoes logical assumptions. Chaloupka writes, "In a cynical era, social discontent transfers itself to widespread, . . . diffuse cynicism. We can no longer assume that adversaries and partners are playing by the rules."[20]

However, not all cynics paint with such broad all-encompassing strokes. There are also focused cynics, individuals whose cynicism is focused on specific targets. They generally claim that they are not cynical by nature, but that they have become cynical about some specific thing—about politics, or even about the rhetoric of one specific politician, about public education, about corporate America or organized labor, or whatever the case may be. But cynicism today is very virulent. Once one perceives the falseness of one sacred icon, the rest quickly become transparent, and the focused cynic usually joins the cynical masses.

Mass Cynicism

The idea of diffuse or "mass" cynicism runs contrary to our usual picture of the cynic. Cynicism is not usually considered diffuse, but rather striking; not universal, but individual.[21] Most of us have in mind the picture of the cynic as an outsider, a loner, an independent, a wry individualist, who scoffs at our ideals, often with a dismissive and sarcastically clever critique. However, today cynicism is so pervasive, so ingrained in America, as to have become almost part of our common sense. The result is a widespread infection, which, in its far-reaching grasp, homogenizes individual cynics into a self nourishing national culture of cynicism. This is mass cynicism, a debilitating whole that is far more formidable than the sum of its faceless, brooding, melancholy parts.

Mass cynicism is one of the underlying central themes of Chaloupka's *Everybody Knows*. "The cynical citizen is now a mass figure," he writes. "Despite differences among American cynics, they share a cynical culture."[22] Indeed, Chaloupka's title itself, taken from a popular Leonard Cohen song of the same title, points to this theme.

In his *Critique of Cynical Reason*, Peter Sloterdijk also has a great deal to say about mass cynicism, which he sees as a part of the Modern Condition. Like routine cynicism, Sloterdijk sees modern mass cynicism as a diffuse "state of consciousness" arising from the "enlightenment" (exposure) of false ideologies. He notes that, although still with us, the bold, "in-your-face" antics of the kynic and the biting individualistic criticism of the independent "outsider cynic" are no longer the norm. The face of modern cynicism is the expressionless, homogeneous face of the masses. Detached, disillusioned, melancholy, the modern citizen cynic withdraws from the stage of action. Today's cynicism "envelops itself in discretion." "The great offensive parades of cynical imprudence have become a rarity; . . . there is no energy left for sarcasm." With the waning of individualism, Sloterdijk observes, modern cynics have "[lost] their sting, and refrain from the risk of letting themselves be put on display. Anonymity now becomes the domain of the cynical devotion." Meanwhile, Sloterdijk reminds us, cynics in power have infiltrated every high office. "They hold key social positions in boards, parliaments, commissions, executive councils, publishing companies, practices, facilities, and lawyers and editor's offices have long been a part of this diffuse cynicism."[23]

Sloterdijk's definitions are echoed and then modified by Timothy Bewes in his *Cynicism and Postmodernity*. Bewes agrees that modern cynicism is a "condition of disillusion," and he adds that it can appear as "a temperament of aestheticism, or even nihilism." "Cynicism is a matter of the individual's relationship to society at large," Bewes tells us, and unlike the ancient variety, which "favored gestural rhetoric over conventional discussion," the modern variety "denotes a refusal to engage with the world as much as a disposition of antagonism towards it, a flight into solitude and interiority. . . ."[24]

But mass cynicism has yet another face beyond that of the withdrawn, disillusioned citizen cynic and the manipulating cynic in power. This is the very modern cynicism of the sort Sloterdijk calls "matter-of-factness." It is the cynicism of indifference, and it is generated by our modern world, our fast-paced mechanized lives, our cities, and most of all by our media. Walter Rathenau in his *On the Critique of the Times* (1912) lays out the case beautifully:

Labor is no longer the activity of life, no longer an accommodation of the body and the soul to the forces of nature, but a thoroughly alien activity . . ., an accommodation of the body and the soul to the mechanism. . . . (And yet) the intellect, still shaking from the excitements of the day, insists on staying in motion, on experiencing a new contest of impressions, with the proviso that these impressions should be more burning and acidic than those that have been gone through. . . . Entertainments of a sensational kind arise, hasty, banal, pompous, fake and poisoned. These border on despair. . . . But even in these insanities and over-stimulations there is something mechanical. The human . . . has surrendered his or her quantum of energy to the flywheel of the world's activity.[25]

In this case cynicism is the product of our surrender to that "mechanical something." But not only are we rendered cynical by Rathenau's "flywheel of the world's activity," at the same time we are rendered unable to sort things out in the order of their importance by the "enormous simultaneity of the media." Sloterdijk explains:

Here, some are eating; there, some are dying. Here some are being tortured; there, famous lovers separate. Here, the "second car" is being discussed; there, a nationwide, catastrophic drought. Here, there are tips on tax write-offs according to section 7b; . . . there, a dead woman lies undiscovered for years in her flat. . . . Such is life. As news, everything is at our disposal. What is foreground; what is background; what is important; what is unimportant; what trend; what episode? Everything is ordered into a uniform line in which uniformity also produces equivalence and indifference.[26]

This too, this indifference, this "matter-of-factness," is modern cynicism, and we are powerless in its grasp. We sense the approaching catastrophe, but we are helpless to do anything about it. T. S. Eliot puts it nicely:

> All twined and tangled together, all are recorded.
> There is no avoiding these things
> And we know nothing of exorcism
> And whether in Argos or in England
> There are certain inflexible laws
> Unalterable, in the nature of music.
> There is nothing at all to be done about it,
> There is nothing to be done about anything.
> And now it is nearly time for the news
> We must listen to the weather report
> And the international catastrophes.
>
> *The Family Reunion*
> T. S. Eliot[27]

Mass cynicism for Sloterdijk is a great deal more than routine, unthinking, or automatic. It is ingrained as a part of the modern consciousness. Cynicism is a natural strategy in the struggle to endure the numbing alienation, hopelessness, and powerlessness of the modern human condition. It is one of the approaches humans use to cope with the ambiguities of the moral wasteland that is the modern era. Donald Kanter and, Phillip Mirvis put it well in *The Cynical Americans*, "The cynic protects himself by setting himself apart from the world and looking down in a detached way on events and circumstances with a jaundiced eye that predicts the worst." The older, more traditional cynic or kynic used his cynicism like a sword.

The modern cynic uses his cynicism like a shield. The traditional cynicism was active, imprudent, arrogant. The modern cynic is distrustful, detached. The modern cynic is enlightened, and he thus has no illusions. But Sloterdijk points out that enlightenment has proved disappointing, and he can no longer bask in its light because his instinct to survive continually motivates him to "act against his better knowledge." Thus, he finds himself trapped in that perpetual "twilight" where "cynicism crystallizes." With this Sloterdijk reveals the true plight of modern cynics. They are "not dumb," he reminds us, and "every now and then they certainly see the nothingness to which everything leads. They know what they are doing and they do it anyway" because the instinct for self-preservation forces them to it. Thus, the "new integrated cynicism" often sees itself as victim, "mourning for 'lost innocence' or for better knowledge."[28]

Causes, Effects, and Techniques of Cynicism

Cynicism is a form of consciousness, a philosophy, a state of mind. Thus a complete definition of it must rely heavily on the academic and theoretical languages of modern philosophy and psychology. For the layman, this kind of obscure scholarly jargon can be difficult, confusing, intimidating, or even just plain unintelligible. In their efforts to clarify matters, many popular writers, thinkers, and pundits turn to the principal techniques and causes or effects of cynicism for their definitions. The idea is that if one knows the cause of (or the reaction to) something, then one will glean great insight into that something. Although this may be a bit indirect, it is a valid approach, for it allows a definition to be rooted in real-world language and not in the language of metaphysics. Also it is important to note that different kinds of cynicism arise from different causes, manifest different strategies, and produce different effects. So, even though chapters 8 and 9 contain detailed discussions of the causes and effects of cynicism in modern American life, it is useful here to briefly pause and consider them. Without them, we would have only a partial understanding of the word.

To begin with, let us consider what we shall call the "standard" definition of the modern cynic: "One who shows a disposition to disbelief in the sincere goodness of human motives and actions, and is wont to express this by sneers and sarcasm."[29]

Cynicism is indeed a disposition, but here its is defined first by its effect, "disbelief," and then by its technique, "sneers and sarcasm." This is a serviceable but incomplete definition, for it points to the responses of the "disposition" without fully defining its nature. Take another example. William Chaloupka defines cynicism as "a condition of lost belief."[30] Here we find a "condition" that is defined by its cause, "lost belief." Again this is accurate and very useful, but incomplete.

Peter Sloterdijk attempts to approach this kind of description from two sides. In his discussions of mass cynicism, the modern human conditions of isolation, detachment, powerlessness, and alienation are part of the definition. They are both causes and effects of modern cynicism. To fend off rising societal alienation and powerlessness, the cynic dons the protective shield of cynicism. He withdraws from the stage of belief and action, and he thus becomes further isolated and detached, more powerless and more alienated. The cycle then begins again.

In the end, Sloterdijk does offer a more complete definition of cynicism. He calls it "enlightened false consciousness," and he takes about 500 pages to explain what he means by this provocative term.

Enlightened False Consciousness

Peter Sloterdijk's *Critique of Cynical Reason* is a valiant effort to fashion a proper definition of modern cynicism, but it often finds itself lost in the quagmire of contradictions that is the modern human condition. Sloterdijk himself admits that his definition is a paradox. How can something be false when it is enlightened? Indeed, the insightful method here is to reconsider our notions of both false consciousness and enlightenment.

The term *false consciousness* recalls the dialectic of Karl Marx. Put simply, "most of what passes for social cognition— the errors, biases, distortion found in human thinking—is essentially the . . . study of false consciousness."[31] Marx saw false consciousness as those "beliefs and values held by individuals and groups" that act to "conceal and mystify what is really going on the world."[32] For Marx, "the acquiescence of the working classes to capitalism was attributable to false consciousness."[33]

Enlightenment is a much more familiar concept. To enlighten means, to "give intellectual or spiritual understanding to; impart knowledge to; free from ignorance, false beliefs or prejudice." It is most often associated with the power of reason. But Sloterdijk casts enlightenment in a new light. As Andreas Huyssen so artfully puts it, Sloterdijk confronts us with the question, "How can one remain an *Aufklärer* [enlightened person] if the enlightenment project of disenchanting the world and freeing it from myth and superstition must indeed be turned against enlightened rationality itself?"[34]

At this point the paradox in Sloterdijk's definition appears indestructible. But in the madness of today's world, everything is destructible. According to Sloterdijk, enlightenment is not always complete; its light shines on some things, but it merely reflects off others, leaving a kind of shadowland, an insecure, frightening twilight world which breeds cynicism. The shadowy light of modern enlightenment is enough to reveal the appalling falsehood of our social consciousness, but we are not free to act upon its disturbing revelations. We are victims of "the nature of things as they are." We are bound by our instinct toward survival to go on as if we did not know the truth, even though we do. We are forever destined to act against our better knowledge because such an act would be world-shattereing. This is the horror of enlightened false consciousness; the horror that is cynicism. In Sloterdijk's words, cynicism is "that modern, unhappy consciousness upon which enlightenment has labored both successfully and in vain. It has learned its lessons in enlightenment, but it has not, and probably was not able to, put them into practice. Well-off and miserable at the same time, this consciousness is no longer affected by any critique of ideology. . . ." In a similar vein, Heinrich Niehues-Probsting defines cynicism as, "the danger of reason perverted, reason turning into irrationality and madness, reason being frustrated because of its own far too exhaled expectations."[35]

If this is modern cynicism, then we are in a world of trouble, but then, of course, we already knew that. Heretofore the enemies of enlightenment have been three: superstition, error, and ignorance. Today there is a fourth: cynicism, the insidious child of our age, which may eventually prove even more ruinous than any of its triplet siblings. Sloterdijk is compelling:

> From the very bottom, from the declassed, urban intelligentsia, and from the very top, from the summits of statesmanly consciousness, signals penetrate serious thinking, signals that provide evidence of a radical, ironic treatment of ethics and of social conventions, as if universal laws existed only for the stupid, while that fatally clever smile plays on the lips of those in the know. More precisely, it is the powerful who smile this way, while the . . . plebeians let out a satirical laugh.[36]

3

The American Dream

> The problems of the world cannot possibly be solved by skeptics and cynics whose horizons are limited by the obvious realities. We need men who can dream of things that never were.
>
> *John Keats*

The twisted smile that plays on the lips of the growing legions of American cynics was painted by a shattered dream. Today, as America's dreams buckle under the weight of so many modern dilemmas, Americans are finding their once unshakable national faith uprooted and their cherished ideals reduced to so many empty platitudes. Yet they cling tenaciously to the very dream that stealthily betrays so many of them. Why? The idea of the American Dream has become a familiar part of modern American life and parlance, but few of us stop to consider its exact nature. Has our national dream changed with the times? Is it still attainable? In order to answer these questions, we must first inventory the dream itself. What are its constituent parts, and how do they work together and relate to the whole?

Many will say that the American Dream defies definition; that it is too vague or too diverse; that it means too many different things to too many different people; that too many different authors have approached it from far too many different directions. What is more, the Dream presents a moving target; a constantly evolving national vision, it goes far back and deep into in our national psyche. An odd combination of Renaissance humanism and Enlightenment individualism, the Dream came to America with the first European settlers. It was then fashioned into something uniquely American.

In 1717, the New England Churchman John Wise called on government to promote "happiness for all," along with "life, liberty, estate and honor." In 1776, Jefferson would confirm this with his "inalienable rights" including the "pursuit of happiness." In 1790, William Dunlap, an American playwright, came closer to the modern definition of the Dream when he extolled "liberty, science, plenty, and country." Fredrick Carpenter insists that whatever else the American dream may be, its two constants are "progress and democracy." It is generally agreed that James Truslow Adams originally coined the term in his 1931 history, *The American Epic*. For Adams, the American Dream was that "life should be better and richer and fuller for everyman." In *The Promise of America*, John Morton Blum lists "social mobility, the prudential values and universal education; land, free government, free thought, and human dignity; economic plenty and industrial power." In *A Visionary Nation*, Zachary Karabell takes a unique approach. He calls America "a layer cake of its previous stages," and he goes on to define the vision (or dream) of each stage: religion, individualism, unity, expansion, government, the market, the Internet, and the future.[1]

The list of components is seemingly endless, but whatever we perceive the individual parts of the Dream to be doesn't really matter. What matters is the overall idea. Regardless of its parts, there always emerges a recognizable whole. What makes the American Dream so powerful is the fact that it is always greater than the sum of its parts. Regardless of the items on the laundry list of ideologies—liberty, democracy, freedom, equality—regardless of the items on the shopping list of material abundance—money, home, car, job, security, education—the result is always the same. Wealth, social status, esteem, equality, security, power, self-fulfillment, celebrity, a better life, all are part of the American Dream. It is a dream of hope—realistic, reasonable hope, embodying "not only aspirations but also avenues by which it can be realized." It is a "set of tenets about achieving success, … the enduring notion that even those who are poor and have limited skills can succeed." It is about credible, present opportunity. The American Dream is simply that we will be free to rise. Without it, cynicism prevails.[2]

The New Land, Individualism, and the American Dream

The American Dream was built on the rough foundation of American individualism, a revolutionary substance unlike anything the world had seen before. Although its seeds were European, its fruit was the product of the new land itself.

In all cultures, there exists a primal myth relating to a journey to a place outside the world, an encounter with some new source of power followed by a life-enhancing return.[3] Most of these stories perpetuate the "myth of the garden" in which the hero discovers an otherworldly, idyllic, pastoral world, an "oasis of harmony, peace and joy." For the Western World, this mythical place has had many names, Arcadia, Atlantis, Avalon, Hesperides, the Blessed Isles, Eden. Beginning in the sixteenth century, the discovery of the New World added flesh to what had theretofore been only fable. The prospect of "withdrawing from the great world and beginning a new life in a fresh green landscape" dazzled the Old World,[4] and Europeans flocked to the new land in increasing numbers. In *The Great Gatsby,* F. Scott Fitzgerald beautifully describes the impact of the new land on the first settlers:

. . . a fresh, green breast of the new world. Its . . .

trees . . . pandered in whispers to the last and greatest of all human dreams; . . . man . . . held his breath
in the presence of this continent, compelled into
an aesthetic contemplation he neither understood
nor desired, face to face for the last time in history
with something commensurate to his capacity for
wonder.[5]

Once landed in the New World, these immigrants found
themselves face to face with the overwhelming fact of the
American frontier, a place where the "bonds of custom are
broken and unrestraint is triumphant." For almost 400 years,
the American frontier represented "escape from the bonds of
the past, . . . scorn for older society," impatience for its restraints and indifference to its lessons. As the new nation grew,
the frontier constantly beckoned, finally offering escape to
the "garden" for the teeming masses that toiled in America's
first industrial cities.[6]

The unfathomable vastness of the new land became a
dream unto itself. In the nineteenth century, "the wildest dream
of Boston was the fact of San Francisco." In his *Letters from an
American Farmer*, the late eighteenth century French immigrant,
Hector St. Jean de Crèvecoeur, writes of the self-reliant settlers on the American frontier. From their unique and sturdy
economic individualism "he deduces the natural emergence
of a new American philosophy that differentiates the colonial
from the European peasant." This new "philosophy" was a
uniquely American brand of frontier individualism—coarse,
strong, acute, inquisitive, practical, quick on the uptake, lacking in art, but "powerful to effect great ends." It is what
Frederick Jackson Turner described as a "dominant individualism working for both good and evil."[7]

The frontier transformed the raw clay of the emerging
American mind, and despite its passing, lingering visions of a

new land and a new life persist in the American Dream today. It is a dream that was built on the shoulders of robust individualism. Sadly, the forces of industrialism that today threaten American individualism have transformed the old "bucolic image of America"[8] into something more akin to a reverie than an an aspiratation. But American individualism persists, although, with its emphasis on self-reliance and mistrust of authority, the American brand of individualism subtily exhibits a few of the same features as cynicism.[9]

The Two Faces of the American Dream

From its very beginning, and in almost every sense of the word, the American Dream has embodied all of the multifold aspects of dreams. It has alternatively appeared as a hope, an aspiration, a goal, a reverie, a vision, a delight, a fantasy, a hallucination, an illusion, and a delusion. But whatever its manifestation, it has tended to divide itself into two distinct parts: the idealistic Dream and the materialistic Dream. The epic of American history can be told as the ongoing struggle to reconcile these two faces of the American Dream.

The idealistic Dream aspired to liberty, justice, democracy, freedom, equality, and self-realization, while the material side aspired to wealth, material success, and property. In the beginning the idealistic side of the Dream was ascendant, and the material side modest. This young American Dream was pastoral—"the simple life," the land, the Jeffersonian vision of a nation of farmers all endowed with "republican virtue." But as the nineteenth century unfolded, the material side of the Dream gained momentum, and the battle began. It is a battle that still rages today. As Daniel Yankelovich notes, "Our culture [ideal side] and economy [material side] are on opposite courses: while culture calls for more freedom, the economy calls for constraint." William Clarke has observed that it is "part of the Dream's enduring quality that it has a dual nature." [10]

Not only does the Dream have two sides, the individualism that supports the Dream is also of a divided character. On one hand we have the kind of individualism that the great French chronicler of early American democracy, Alexis de Tocqueville, called "individualism properly understood." This is an individualism focused on "the common good." De Tocqueville believed that in a democracy the private interests of individuals could only be served "when they took care of the overall well-being of society."[11] On the other hand there is individualism that is selfish and inwardly turned. The first kind of individualism leads to successful democracy, the second to tyranny.

As the brief history outlined in chapters 4 through 7 will illustrate, the forces of the idealistic side of the Dream are fragile but resilient, while the forces of the materialistic side are durable but unstable. Historically these two dreams have intermingled both in dances of symbiotic balance and in collisions of all out war. In a perfect world, one supports the other. With de Tocqueville's "individualism properly understood," the ideal side of the Dream—liberty, equality, and democracy—works to create a fertile environment for the growth of the material side just as John Locke and Adam Smith had predicted. While at the same time, the material side provides stability and makes equality and the "pursuit of happiness" a realistic and present hope. De Tocqueville understood this all too well when he wrote, " . . . democracy thrives only if it sees to the universal distribution of hope."[12] De Tocqueville understood the importance of the American Dream.

But we do not live in an ideal world. Today the distribution of hope in America is far from equitable, and the appetites of the material side of the American Dream are far more ravenous than anyone could have predicted. As the modern age advances, the kind of individualism that seeks the common good is being engulfed by an unlovely, acquisitive, grasping individualism that seeks selfish ends. All the while, both are being swallowed up by the monotonous homogeneity of an industrial world, in which individualism is replaced by a shallow sense of well-being and esteem that flows from material possessions and a conforming group consciousness.

The American Dream of Progress

Although the idealistic side of the Dream is often at odds with the material side, there is a place where the two come together to complete the all-embracing American Dream, a vision that, as we have seen, is greater than the sum of its parts. The junction of the ideal and material sides of the Dream is the birthplace of the American dream of Progress. It is more than the American dream of Upward Mobility, more than the observable, measurable progress of economics, social elasticity, or politics. Rather, it is an idealized notion of progress that lies at the heart of our national Dream.

The American dream of Progress has its roots in the Enlightenment concept of the perfectibility of man. American offshoots of this notion are rugged individualism, faith in man's ability to triumph over the land, belief in the greatness of the common man, and a sturdy, moralistic work ethic. As the national experience unfolded, Americans came to believe that hard work, self-denial, endurance, initiative, thrift, patience, industry, sobriety, moderation, and self-discipline paved a road to a better life, and that this road was open to all Americans. At the end of it stood a new American hero, the self-made man. The combination of this idea of the self-made man, frontier individualism, the capitalist myth of enterprise, and America's love affair with the machine as manifested in the power of her industry yields an American dream of Progress that still beckons. At its heart is the notion that, with hard work, material and social progress are inevitable in America.

Over the years the nation's economic progress added

credibility to the idea of perpetually advancing Progress. History not only validated the material side of the Dream, it also bolstered belief in the idealistic side. Indeed, as David Potter writes, "American idealism has often framed its altruistic goals in material terms—for instance, a rising standard of living as a means to a better life. Moreover Americans are committed to the view that materialistic means are necessary to idealistic ends."[13] Here the ideal and the material sides of the Dream meet. As America became increasingly better off materially, her citizens became more convinced that each future generation would be better off than the one before it. In this confident atmosphere of Progress, many assumed that the old ideologies were intact and working.

A host of lesser American dreams support the dream of Progress including the dreams of science, technology, know-how, education, and business creation, to name but a few. In the American mind, hard work and excellence achieved in all of these fields have made the dream of Progress possible. Boastful, arrogant, audacious, blindly nationalistic, and most of all impossible, the American dream of Progress is a visionary Ponzi scheme in which things promise to keep getting better until an American utopia is finally achieved. After that, the Dream might be for a world utopia, built on the American model. Richard T. Gill goes so far as to project that "the prosperity guaranteed by the dream of Progress" is, "in significant measure, a modern substitute for an other-worldly paradise that had come to be seen, by many, as an increasingly doubtful proposition."[14]

Closely related to the American Dream of progress is the American Dream of success, which placed a heavy stress on personal achievement, "especially secular occupational achievement. The 'success story' and the respect accorded the self-made man are distinctly American." The rise from obscurity to success is the archetypical embodiment of the American Dream. This is why Gary Scharhorst has called Horatio Alger "one of the great mythmakers of the modern world."[15] But in America today success is rarely a measure of achievement; it is rather more often a measure of material wealth. The Dream of success is defecting from the idealistic side of the ledger to its materialistic side.

The idea of progress has come a long way from the dream of men at work in the wilderness; from the dream of a fair day's work for a fair day's pay; from the dream that education will ensure a "leg up" on the ladder of success. And yet the American Dream of progress still holds us in its grasp. It is a dream that is bound to disappoint.

The Standardization of the American Dream

As the twentieth century began to unfold and America slowly evolved from a nation of farmers into a modern, industrial mass culture, something happened to the American Dream. All of the old individualisms and all of old the dreams, both idealistic and materialistic, were collected and then simmered and stirred in the great new stew-pot of the gathering modern American consciousness. Tending the great cauldron were the witches of the emerging new media and the kitchen boys of modern advertising. When the cooking period was over, there emerged a new, homogeneous, pre-packaged American Dream ready for nationwide consumption.

Here was the new *Saturday Evening Post* or "television" version of the American Dream that we still cling to today—a squeaky clean dream of Norman Rockwell and "Leave It to Beaver"; an impossible confectionary dream of pithy modern slogans fashioned from the old ideals of liberty, equality, and democracy; a materialistic dream of washing machines and automobiles and toasters, reclining chairs and homes in the suburbs. By the 1950s, the American Dream had been transformed into an American cliché comprised of equal parts motherhood, apple pie, and family values. A Mommy, a Daddy, two-and-a-half children, a comfortable home the suburbs, two cars, a steady job, college educations, a secure future, all were constituent parts of a new, standardized, all-middle-class "national identity," perfectly packaged, easy to digest, and all based on the Dream of progress.

Does the American Dream have relevance today? Does it still have the power to excite? Does it still generate commitment?[16] Or have we given in to a new standardized American Dream, so vapid that it only gives respectful lip service to the old idealistic dreams?

The Arrogance of the American Dream

Almost from the beginning there was something about America that seemed larger than life: the vastness of the land, the breadth of the great ocean that separated America from the Old World, the wildness of the frontier, the tenacious self-reliance and bold utopian dreams of the early settlers, dreams that themselves were larger than life. The virulent strain of individualism that took root and flourished here, coupled with so many early successes in taming the new land, soon led to a boastful national self-confidence that would later create in America an evangelical vision of a nation superior in almost every respect to those her immigrant citizens had left behind. In this vision the government was more equalitarian, the society was more elastic, the economy was more robust, and the people were more industrious than in other nations. In the eighteenth and nineteenth centuries, when Americans looked at Europe, they saw a continent that appeared to buckle under the weight of age-old aristocracies, an outdated mercantilism, and social stagnation.

There is ample evidence that such arrogance was present in America from an early date. John Winthrop envisioned

America as a "City on the Hill," a beacon for the aspirations of "all of Christendom." Later, Jonathan Edwards called forth a vision of colonial American Puritanism as the "glorious renovator of the world." In a similar fashion many of the founding fathers saw the new nation as a kind of universal savior. John Adams wrote, "I have always considered the settlement of America . . . as the opening of a grand scheme . . . for the illumination and emancipation of mankind all over the world."[17] The impossibly grand vision of Yankee ability was clear in America's early mythical heroes. Paul Bunyan and Pecos Bill single-handedly felled great forests and lassoed tornados.

All of this innocent, self-congratulatory idealism, mythmaking, and braggadocio was fine on the frontier, but by the time the nineteenth century drew to a close, America was well on its way to becoming a world power. Her new-found power fueled nationalistic self-righteousness and led to attempts to use America's strength and wealth to impose American ways elsewhere. Some of these attempts were justifiable, but as John Morton Blum writes in *The Promise of America*, "The United States broke its national promise when it placed its own grandeur ahead of the interests of those it helped. It perverted the promise when it followed a course legitimate for its own security in the disingenuous name of someone else's freedom. It violated the promise when it insisted that another country's self-determination adhere to the patterns of the American model."[18]

As the nation grew and prospered in the twentieth century, the myth of American superiority supported the American dream of Progress. The United States of America saw itself as victor over nature, over material wealth, and finally, over other nations—an invulnerable fortress, an unbeatable foe. At the close of the Second World War, the American dream of Progress appeared real, and the possibilities for American know-how, ingenuity, and moxie seemed endless. Underneath it all lay the notion that Americans, with their "can-do" mentality, surpassed all other nations in technical and scientific innovation, in governmental arrangement, in education, in initiative, and in moral fiber. So confident were most Americans of their nation's superiority that the cherished American dream of Progress had come to include the belief that the spread of her revolution—of her systems of governmental, economic, and social organization—was inevitable.[19] In short, the apparent success of the American dream of Progress confirmed what many Americans had suspected almost from the beginning, that America was right and everyone else in the world was wrong; that only America could understand and control history. It was the most provincial of notions, a nightmarish blend of the concepts of individualism and the perfectibility of humankind.

Dreams, Expectations, Promises, Rights, and Entitlements

When America became a nation, Americans recognized certain rights as the just claim of all citizens. Life, liberty, and the pursuit of happiness were thought to be "inalienable," axiomatic—the natural, God-given rights of every man. Later the Bill of Rights laid down laws to further define and to protect these rights. These were not dreams; they were promises, made by a government of the people, to the people. The dream was that the government would keep its promise and establish an environment in which citizens were free to pursue other dreams.

Any effort toward a better life begins with a dream that beckons the dreamer onward toward a goal. Whether for individuals or for nations, the right kind of dreams supply the dreamer with a kind of focused motivational energy. Although a dream may be ambitious, it must entertain at least a reasonable possibility of success. This is to say that the right kind of dream must be promising without being a promise. Only then can it entice and motivate the dreamer.

The American Dream flourished in this atmosphere, and for decades it beckoned its dreamers to new heights. Not everyone achieved his or her dreams, but so many prospered that the dream itself began to change. Expectations soared, and many came to believe that the road to prosperity led endlessly upward. This was the American Dream of progress. This optimistic vision sustained the dreamers for a time. But as its prospects became more and more promising, the dream became more and more like an entitlement until, finally, somewhere in the middle of the twentieth century, many "Americans came to believe that prosperity was their birthright,"[20] with or without the traditional work ethic. The American Dream was becoming the American Promise, and expectations were turning into perceived certainties.

At about the same time, faith began to rise in the capacity of the government to solve social problems. By the late decades of the twentieth century, what earlier generations had considered dreams and later generations had considered privileges, many modern Americans were considering entitlements. The stage was set for an age of uncertainty that would bring disappointment and its faithful follower, cynicism.

The American Dream at the Turn of the Twenty-first Century

The stage was indeed set for disappointment. Just before the twenty-first century began, those Americans who had not already given in to cynicism were either clinging to a watered-down version of the old American Dream of progress, or embracing the new American promise of prosperity. A new American Dream was needed, for no nation can endure without a dream.

But what was the new dream to be? The old Dream no

longer seemed realistic in the modern world. The foundations of individualism upon which it had been built had been eroded by the conformity of the industrial world and by the interdependence of mass society. America was losing her faith in the future. For many, America's most cherished ideals were being transformed into so many vague platitudes or traded for a shallow materialism. Reasons for public mistrust in government went far deeper than the misbehavior of politicians. "The aspirations once represented by the symbol of the ideal landscape" could no longer be "embodied by . . . current institutions."[21] Adherence to the work ethic and the dream of success no longer appeared to yield predictable upward economic and social mobility. The traditional American family was disappearing, and traditional values were adrift in a sea of ambiguity.

What was needed was not more belief in the old dreams, but better, more realistic dreams. One would think that in an age of disappointment, mistrust, and uncertainty, the nation would seek new, modest, more pragmatic dreams, dreams in line with the harsh realities of the times. One would think that Americans would forsake the arrogant dreams of entitlement, the shallow dreams of material wealth, and the unrealistic dream of Progress. But this is not what seems to have happened. The new American Dream is clearly the most unrealistic dream of all: a shallow fantasy of impossible celebrity, gratuitous reward, and unwholesome heroes.

As irrational as this new Dream may appear, when one considers the troubled mind of present-day America, it is not a surprise. Industrialization, urbanization, and the alienations of modern industrialized society have cut Americans off from the soil, transformed a nation of farmers into a nation of clerks, and homogenized society. The result is that the two fundamental, foundational underpinnings of the old American Dream, individualism and the work ethic, have been weakened, if not destroyed. Owing to our long national history of material progress and the unrealistically high expectations of the enormously influential "baby boomer" generation, Americans still believe in the material side of the American Dream of abundance. At the same time, they desperately want to believe in the teetering American Dream of progress that promised that each generation would be better off than the one before it. But that dream no longer seems to deliver, and in the resulting atmosphere of uncertainty, Americans have thrust leisure into the void left by the passing of the work ethic and embraced conformity and celebrity in the place of individualism.

The passing of individualism certainly explains the current American fascination with celebrity. David Marshall writes, ". . . celebrity . . . is the public representation of individuality in contemporary culture." When the individual citizen is robbed of his individualism by the interdependence of modern society, it seems natural that he might seek to vicariously recapture it in the Day-Glo illusions that are the celebrity icons of our modern pop culture. The puppeteers of modern capitalism have been quick to exploit the trend, and today the media shamelessly "hypes" its stars in what Tyler Cowen calls "the commodification of individualism and the individual image." "Fame," says Cowen, "has become the ideological and intellectual fabric of modern capitalism." This is not a new idea. Back in the 1930s and '40s Horkheimer and Adorno published damning critiques of the modern "cult of personality," emphasizing a great "mass deception." The "star," they said, seems to epitomize the potential of everyone in American society, but the reality is that the "star" is part of a "system of false promise in a system of capital, which offers the reward of stardom to a random few in order to perpetuate the myth of potential universal success." Also writing in the 1940s, Leo Lowenthal noted that "whereas in the previous social systems, there had been an emphasis on success based on hard work, in current society . . . the key determinants are luck and circumstance." Twenty years later Herbert Marcuse published his *One Dimensional Man*, in which he reaffirmed Horkheimer and Adorno's ideas and added that not only is celebrity the site of false value, "it serves to place the individual into an acceptance of the modern condition." For Marcuse, modern society has become a powerful instrument of domination, in which consumerism, celebrity, and the media combine to generate "false needs" that narrowly define our consciousness and pacify our inclinations to social and political action. In America, the rickety foundations of celebrity and luck have today been accepted as replacements for the old frontier individualism and the Puritan work ethic that once so securely supported much of the weight of the full-blown American dream.[22]

The erosion of the work ethic has led modern Americans to seek broader substitute foundations to shore up their teetering dreams. Where hard work once defined the path to self-fulfillment in America, today many seek self-realization in leisure and in a modern fantasy world of shallow entertainments and contrived amusements—a world of television, celebrity, sports, cyberspace, malls and theme parks. For these modern consumers, work has become a means to these ends, not an end in itself as it was for their forbearers. Given the fact that the old work ethic "no longer fits the facts" of modern American life[23] and considering the uncertainty manifest in the current state of affairs, it is not surprising that many Americans have chosen short-term solutions "involving sensual gratification." Such solutions "undermine the tolerance for hard work needed to achieve long-term goals."[24] Max Lerner describes the current scene well:

> The pull of property, no longer in tools and productive land but in consumer goods; the sense of

power and pleasure in the means of sight and sound and movement placed at his disposal by the communications revolution; the glorying in what seems to make the world of drama and entertainment accessible; the whole of popular culture; the feeling of access to new gradients of income and experience; these form the new soil in which America has found its roots.[25]

Many Americans today take affluence for granted, and millions no longer turn to work for self-fulfillment. Many feel trapped, and some have mortgaged their lives. Most are fascinated by celebrity. The nation is sorely in need of new dreams. But the flashy, new, plastic dreams with which America is today experimenting are not likely to outdo the old dreams, nor are they likely fill the void left by the passing of individualism and the work ethic. In fact, the new American Dream may not be a dream at all, but rather an escape—an escape into consumerism, fads, leisure, entertainment, and celebrity—stimulations that require no serious response. It is a shallow vision indeed in which "impressions overshadow achievements and the images and symbols of success are more important than the actual achievement."[26]

Part II:

The Evolution of the American Dream and the Changing Face of Cynicism in America

Cynicism never appears in a vacuum; it has a reason, a history.

Ronald C. Arnett and Pat Arneson

4

The Origins of the American Dream, 1492–1800

The complex visions that make up the American Dream have both Old World and New World origins, and they can be fully explained by neither alone. For Europeans of the sixteenth century the New World itself appeared to be a kind of dream. Early reports of a great green wilderness beyond the sea quickly awakened ancient poetic visions of a distant Arcadian garden, a theretofore-mythical land where one might shed the past and begin life anew. To this dream-like wilderness European colonists brought the evolving notions that were to later form the foundations for the American Dream. Successive European influences include Renaissance humanism, English Independency, the revolutionary doctrine of natural rights, French Romantic theory, the explosion of scientific knowledge and the new capitalistic economic order along with the sweeping social changes that followed in its wake. These and other European ingredients were imported to a pristine America fascinated by utopian ventures and new experiments in government.[1] Everything was then slowly cooked in the crude cauldron of a new continent while the vast new land added its own unique, frontier ingredients to strongly flavor an already complex brew. The American Dream would simmer for over 300 years.

European Background, 1492–1607

The Renaissance. When Christopher Columbus first set foot in the New World the footings that would support the

American Dream were already being laid. In 1492 the spirit that inspired Columbus was beginning to spread in Europe. The new spirit did not confine itself to global exploration. It blossomed into scientific inquiries of all sorts. While Columbus sailed, new theories of the heavens were being formulated. New laws for the physical world were about to be put forth, and new inventions like movable type and the telescope were about to appear. Nor did the spirit confine itself to scientific endeavors.

A new unifying political impulse was loose in Europe as national states replaced feudal institutions. An upwardly mobile urban bourgeoisie was forging a new social order driven by a new capitalistic system of economics, and audacious new Protestant religious reformers were about to denounce the once rigid authority and dogma of the Roman Catholic Church. All of these forces together would become the raw materials from which America would eventually build her dreams, but the construction period was to be long and fraught with adversity.

At the heart of the Renaissance spirit that drove Columbus beat the revolutionary pulse of individualism. The secular Renaissance fashion of revisiting the intellectual legacy of the Classical world gave shape to a new vision of mankind called humanism. It would be the perfection of this European ideal of the rights and worth of the individual, transported to the New World and then reshaped by the new land itself, that would eventually become the center-post of the American Dream.

Set against medieval Catholicism's dreary dogma, humanism was truly revolutionary. The doctrine of the Church was original sin. The doctrine of humanism was original goodness. Dark Age Catholicism was based on harsh visions of the world as merely an unpleasant stopover where souls are judged for eternity. Humanists, on the other hand, thought that "the body and soul are one, and that the actions of the body naturally and fittingly express the humanity of the soul."[2]

The Reformation. By the time Columbus returned from his last voyage in 1504, the Reformation was only 15 years away, and when Martin Luther nailed his 95 theses to the door of the Wittenberg Cathedral in 1519, he unleashed upon the face of Europe the relentless hounds that would only be sated by the meat of liberty. Thus, it was Martin Luther, himself, who helped to lay the foundation for the American Dream, and it was the cynicism and scoffing attitudes he observed in the Church leadership in Rome that drove Luther to his rebellion.

There can be no doubt that Luther's sympathies were with the humanists, but he was not interested in secular matters. He was interested only in preaching a religion of piety. Still, his rebellion was bold, and his incendiary words fired issues far beyond his strictly religious intent. In his *Treatise on Christian Liberty,* Luther wrote, " . . . neither pope nor bishop nor any other man has the right to impose a single syllable of law upon a Christian man without his consent; and if he does, it is done in the spirit of tyranny." He was talking about church law only. He believed that Christian faith had nothing to do with politics.[3]

After the Reformation began, Luther spent the rest of his life trying to "erect a dam of absolute religious authority to hold back the religious, economic and political forces he had let loose." But the situation was beyond his control. His fiery words and audacious rebellion had ignited an intense "spirit of uncompromising individualism that would eventually espouse the principle of democracy in church and state." Luther originated Protestantism, the right to protest, and it opened the way for other protests, one of which was to create the United States of America and all of her various dreams.[4]

But the progress of the dream was not to be linear.

While Luther's protest inspired forward-thinking, New Testament, individualistic notions of liberty, John Calvin's Old Testament authoritarian theories were at odds with liberty. Calvin's thinking was fundamentally cynical. This is to say that he saw too little good in human nature to trust government to any broad constituency. As John Fiske so aptly puts it, Calvinists "showed no tendency toward freedom of thought, but rather a bigotry quite as intense as that which animated the system against which they fought."[5] That American Puritanism was generally of a Calvinist rather than a Lutheran strain was a misfortune that greatly hindered the cause of liberty in America. It was the Calvinist leanings of New England Puritanism that for a time stood directly across the path that led to the American Dream.

English Independency and the Puritans. By the time of the Puritan exodus from England to America about 100 years after Luther nailed up his 95 theses in Wittenberg, European, and specifically, English, Puritanism had become quite diverse. Its ranks had become splintered even though all Puritans believed in a simple path to God, free from Catholic and Anglican ceremony, church organization, and pomp. At one end of the spectrum were the forces of oligarchic Calvinist Presbyterianism and at the other were those loyal to democratic Independency, an offshoot radical branch of Puritanism. Nonetheless, all the factions of English Puritanism found it necessary to join together in support of the cause of religious toleration in England, and so even the most conservative of Calvinists found himself on the liberal side of the aisle when it came to opposing the Stuart monarchy's oppression of Puritans in England and the crown's struggles to establish the divine right of kings and secure national doctrinal unity under the roof of the Church of England. It was the fusion of these last two elements, one political and one religious, that led to the English Civil War. But by the time Cromwell's New Model Army rode into battle, twenty thousand English Puritans had fled to America.[6] With them they carried the seeds of the American Dream.

Ironically Cromwell's victory over the king lead to the ill-fated English Commonwealth. Cromwell himself dictatorially wielded the power of state under the Protectorate until his death and the subsequent restoration of the Stuart monarchy. It was a reactionary end for such a liberal epic. Still, Cromwell's victory had "shattered the monarchal power in England at a time when monarchal power was bearing down all opposition in the other great countries of Europe."[7] It also introduced for the first time an army composed of ordinary citizens fighting for ideological reasons, a precedent that would have effects that reached all the way to colonial America.[8] Already, across the Atlantic, Puritanism was slowly becoming "the cutting edge that hewed liberty, democracy, humanitarianism and education out of . . . the American Wilderness."[9]

The Early Colonial Period, 1607–1700
The Puritans in New England. The Congregational, Presbyterian, Methodist, Baptist, Unitarian, Quaker, and other protestant sects of the United States are offshoots of seventeenth century English and Scottish Puritanism.[10] But despite its religious underpinnings, Puritanism contributed much to the evolving political, social, and economic design for the framework that was to later support the American Dream.

The first Puritan settlements in New England certainly did not appear to be the forbearers of any future American dreams of liberty and democracy. They were ruled by oligarchic theocracies, and their only law was God's law as interpreted and enforced by a small group of magistrates. But this system eventually met with opposition, and in the end Puritan

Independency won out over strict Calvinist oligarchy. The theory and practice of Independency implies two fundamental rights: "1) the right of the individual to determine his own belief and 2) the right to join with others in the institutional expression and spread of these beliefs." Within its "theocratic fascination, and in words as arrogant as ever fell from priestly lips, there was couched the assertion of the popular will against despotic privilege." In colonial America these ecclesiastical notions slowly shifted to the fields of politics and economics to form the main pillars of the American Dream.[11]

The Early Colonial Frontier. It is significant to note that liberal democratic principles did not initially come from the Massachusetts Bay Colony, which remained strongly conservative. They came rather from Connecticut and Rhode Island Puritans out on the edge of what was then the frontier. In these wild places, the American wilderness was at work molding a new brand of individualism, whose self-reliant converts dreamed more liberal dreams. Here for the first time we see the frontier inspiring bold escapes from the bondage of the past.

While John Winthrop of Massachusetts was insisting that the multitude was "incapable of governing wisely,"[12] Thomas Hooker of Hartford was asserting that, "the foundation of authority is laid, firstly, in the free consent of the people."[13] And Roger Williams of Rhode Island was preaching the same sermon: "The sovereign power of all civil authority is founded in the consent of the people. . . ."[14] Here, very early on, we can see the importance of the frontier in the shaping of the American Dream as, even in the 1630s, the American frontier was becoming "productive of individualism." And from the very beginning the rugged individualism forged on the American frontier has "promoted democracy." "On the frontier," writes the American historian Frederick Jackson Turner, "the bonds of custom are broken and unrestraint is triumphant." Turner saw the frontier as "a great escape from the bondage of the past," producing "scorn for the older society, . . . impatience in its restraints and ideas, and indifference to its lessons." "Individualist and democratic tendencies were emphasized . . . by wilderness conditions," Turner wrote.[15] The new land and the harsh realities of the frontier forged a new uniquely American spirit—the self-reliant assurance we call democratic individualism.

Jamestown. Despite its idealist beginnings, the American Dream contained a material side as well, and it, too, was erected on the firm foundations of individualism. The Puritans had brought with them not only their robust work ethic, but also a healthy respect for thrift and for the accumulation of wealth. Not coincidentally, both Plymouth and Jamestown were founded and first overseen by private investment companies, not by the English crown.

The seeds that would later blossom to become the material side of the American Dream were planted very early on at Jamestown. Although all the land we now call Virginia was originally owned by The Virginia Company and worked by tenants, it was not long before it was decided that after seven years of service tenants were to be given the land outright. This greatly increased productivity, and by the late 1620s large plantations stretched a full twenty miles inland along the James River. Meanwhile the company had been "quick to order the abolishment of arbitrary rule, introduce English common law and due process, encourage private property, and summon a representative assembly."[16] As would eventually become the case in New England, almost from the beginning the settlers at Jamestown sought a government of laws, not of men. Jamestown is an early example of colonial America's determination to live under the rule of law. Elsewhere, European colonists lived under the rule of the prince or his representative.

As the American experience unfolded, English colonists continued to import the seeds of the American Dream from Europe and scatter them in the wilderness of a new land. The result was a dual harvest: a dream of liberty *and* a dream of property. These two dreams would later clash as, over and over again, the champions of broad individual rights attempted to scale the barricades of the defenders of property rights.

The Late Colonial Period, 1700–1763
Eighteenth Century Settlement in America. At the dawn of the eighteenth century, the American colonies were emerging bloodied but victorious from a series of nasty Indian Wars, and the frontier was expanding westward to the Great Lakes in the north and to the edge of Appalachians farther south. New colonies were appearing, and elective assemblies were soon functioning in every one of them. Religious excess was diminishing everywhere, and immigrants were pouring in. In 1700 the population of the English colonies in American was between one hundred thousand and three hundred thousand. By the time the Declaration of Independence was signed the population of English Colonial America would be above two and a half million.[17] As the great kettle of American individualism was heated, the dreams that simmered inside began to solidify and take on form.

The new immigrants were a diverse, ragtag lot, "a rude flux of the disillusioned and disinherited of Europe." The American Dream was no longer for Englishmen alone, it beckoned to Scots, Irish, and, later, to settlers from the continent. According to Parrington most of these were men who "wrote little, debated little and very likely thought little."[18] Still, undaunted by hardship, they penetrated the wilderness and set it under the plow. Despite their ethnic diversity and drab insularity, in them was growing something of great importance:

the psychology of American individualism that would form the underpinning of the American Dream. Parrington waxes eloquent on the subject:

> . . . a vast drama, magnificent in the breath and sweep of its movement, was being enacted by players unconscious of their parts. Not until long after they had gone to their graves were the broad lines of that drama revealed. Today it is plain that those unremembered years were engaged in clearing away encumbrances more significant that the great oaks and maples of the virgin wilderness: they were uprooting ancient habits of thought, destroying social customs that had grown old and dignified in class-ridden Europe. A new philosophy was being created by the wide spaces that was to be enormously significant when it came to self-consciousness.[19]

There is perhaps no better original account of the progress of the American Dream in this late colonial era than that given by the Frenchman and eighteenth-century colonial democrat de Crèvecoeur in his *Letters from an American Farmer*. De Crèvecoeur came to America in 1760. Of European colonial pioneers and farmers he writes:

> . . . everything tended to regenerate them, new laws, new mode of living, new social system; here they were become men; in Europe they were as so many useless plants . . . withered and mowed down by want, hunger and war. By what invisible power has this surprising metamorphosis been performed? By that of the laws of their industry . . . his country is that which gives him land, bread, protection, and consequence. . . . Here the rewards of his industry

> follow in equal steps with the progress of his labor;
> his labor is founded on the basis of nature, self-
> reliance; can it want a stronger allurement?[20]

Here is enthusiastic testament to what his contemporary, English philosopher John Locke, called "clearing the ground of . . . rubbish" so that the new man might start from scratch to build new dreams in his own new world.

Indeed these immigrants nurtured the infant American Dream with their everyday experiences of the new land. And they were nourished by it. It was a rational process just like the process Locke described; that is to say, it was knowledge gained from experience. Back in Europe, Locke was brewing a philosophical stew of his own, a recipe for a new Age of Reason and Enlightenment. From Locke's recipe the colonists would borrow an abundance of potent ingredients to strengthen the great American stew they were brewing in the American backwoods.

The Age of Reason in Europe. The first two English monarchs after the end of Cromwell's Protectorate in 1660 did not last long, and neither did the crown's continued quarrels with Parliament. In 1688, James II was banished to France, and William and Mary marched into London and on to the English throne. Thereafter all power was centered in Parliament. The new monarchs reaffirmed the declaration of rights with a new bill of rights curtailing royal power, providing for frequent, free parliamentary elections and for free speech, and forbidding Catholics to ascend to the throne. Not long afterward the Toleration Act became English law, granting freedom of worship to all Protestant dissenters.

Two years after William and Mary were crowned, John Locke published his *Essay Concerning Human Understanding*. Building on the science of Newton and the empiricism of

Hobbes as well as on his own ideas of natural law, Locke sought to understand how we come to know things. He proposed that reason was the key; that the human mind was a blank page (a *tabula rasa*) to be written on by experience. He also described ways to knowledge beyond experience, including demonstrative, sensitive, and intuitive knowledge, the concept of which resounds in the American Declaration of Independence in its reference to "inalienable rights." He later published his *Two Treatises on Government* in which he concluded that "government is freely created by the people to protect already existing rights, and it derives its power from 'the consent of the governed.'"[21]

Around 1730, French philosophers began to embrace the ideas of Newton and Locke and carried them "beyond their development in England." The most resounding of these voices was that of Voltaire. Like Luther, Voltaire did not intend to incite political revolution, but his ideas were more powerful than he thought. Firmly rooted in the empiricism of Locke and in the doubting methods of Descartes and Pascal, Voltaire's reason was explosive, "exposing for all to see the evils of state, society, and religion." If we add to this Montesquieu's idea of the separation of powers and Rousseau's notion of the social contract, we have much of the intellectual underpinning for both the Declaration of Independence and the United States Constitution. These European ideas were not part of the American Dream. They were the philosophical supports that would hold it firmly in the howling winds of the coming storm.[22]

The Age of Reason in the American Colonies.
The early 1700s saw theocracy and the political power of religious leaders, once so powerful in New England, crumbling before the onslaught of more liberal ideas. Typical of the many dissenters who championed the new way of thinking was the

Rev. John Wise of Ipswich. In 1717 Wise published his *Vindication of the Government of the Church of New England* in which he wrote, "The end of all good government is to cultivate humanity, and promote the happiness of all, and the good of every man in his rights, his life, his liberty, estate, honor etc., without injury or abuse to any." Wise was clearly familiar with the writings of John Locke, for in the same work he added, "A democracy in church or state, is a very honorable and regular government according to the dictates of right and reason."[23] In fact the application of reason resulted in a universal lessening of religious zeal. When measured by the yardstick of reason, religious fervor was regarded as untrustworthy, a dubious reliance on emotional processes, and thus an abdication of reason.[24]

Meanwhile the new immigrants that were pouring into the English American colonies dreamed other dreams that were neither spiritual nor political in nature; they were almost wholly economic.[25] Reports of free land and limitless opportunity in America drove the dispossessed of Europe to America's shores and then inland to the edge of the frontier. With this generation of "pilgrims" came a new, materialistic American Dream that has endured to this day. Locke kindled this new American Dream as well as the older dream of liberty when he penned his *Two Treatises on Government,* "The state of nature has a law of nature to govern it which obliges everyone; and reason, which is that law, teaches all mankind who will consult it that, being all equal and independent, no one ought to harm another in his life, health, liberty or possessions."[26]

The Great Awakening. Despite the gathering voices of reason and the decline of church power and influence, eighteenth century colonial America was still populated by godly men, and around 1740 a broad-based religious revival began. It was called the Great Awakening. Inspired by the fiery sermons of Jonathan Edwards and George Whitfield, American colonists by the thousands rededicated themselves to the simple path to God that had, from the beginning, stood at the center of Puritan theology. But this time there was a difference. "The Great Awakening pushed the church aside and left the individual to stand alone before God's judgment." This not only stimulated religious zeal but also "gave the common man an increased sense of significance and thus indirectly contributed to the American Revolution." Although spiritual in nature, the Great Awakening had an effect in secular affairs, fanning the flames of individualism that burned beneath the cauldron of the simmering the American Dream.[27]

The Revolutionary Period, 1763–1800

The American Revolution. In the decade before the Revolution, separatist feelings were not particularly strong in the American colonies. Every colony had a large degree of self-determination, and in general men were free to pursue their interests as they saw fit. "Of social unrest, the common fuel of revolutions, there was practically none." Although the colonists felt that they were entitled to all the constitutional rights that Englishmen enjoyed and despite Parliament's increasing blundering, most remained reluctant to face a choice between their loyalty to the British Empire and their love of their newfound native land. Inherent in this reluctance was a widespread fear of democratic forms of government that lingered despite the oratory of men like Samuel Adams, who declared, "The fear of the people's abusing their liberty is an argument against their having the enjoyment of it." Throughout the revolutionary period many Americans continued to cynically believe that all democracies would quickly give way to anarchy. In such a skeptical climate, it took radical leaders ten years after the Stamp Act to decide that the colonies were not bound by British law. In the end the American Revolution was as much a result of a "short-sighted English imperialism" as any long-smoldering dreams of "liberty and the pursuit of happiness."[28]

Nonetheless, as the clouds of revolution gathered, the embers of the American Dream of liberty were still glowing, and once the fighting started they were quick to ignite. Revolutionary leaders swiftly discovered that "if their cause were to make any headway, appeal must . . . rest on philosophical rather than legal grounds," and as the crisis developed, colonial sentiment quickly crystallized and asserted its republican purpose. As John Adams later put it, "The Revolution was in the mind of the people."[29]

And so was the American Dream. After simmering for almost 170 years, the American Dream seemed to suddenly materialize, and a new breed of American patriots began using lofty words like "*liberty, freedom, rights, republic, independence, and equality.*"[30] After Lexington and Concord, many Americans had quickly ceased to view these as vague abstractions. "They meant first freedom under laws of their own making, and second the right to do anything that did not harm another."[31] "The language of liberty and rights was English, and it drew directly or indirectly from the Magna Carta, the writings of John Locke, and the heritage of the English Civil War."[32] Ironically, in 1775, it seemed that all America had to do to get on with her dreams was defeat the English.

The Declaration of Independence. After Lexington and Concord, almost fourteen months elapsed before the Declaration of Independence was drafted and signed. Meanwhile fighting began in earnest while Americans remained divided. Samuel Eliot Morison estimates that while only 10% of the colonial population remained loyal to England, only 40% were active patriots, and a full half were undecided and

thus neutral. The New England countryside remained suspicious of seaport agitators, and the backcountry from Virginia to the Carolinas was "slow to catch fire. . . ."[33]

In fact the backcountry had a long history of grievances against the colonial capitals, and this translated into a certain amount of cynicism when it came to these pioneers' stake in what appeared to many westerners to be a coastal intellectual's war. Still, the native experience of the backcountry, and of all colonials for that matter, was individualism. The self-governing state had so long been established in the colonies as to be viewed as a natural right. The political compact "had taken form in American thought a generation before Locke gave currency to the theorem, and Jefferson was expressing native conclusions drawn from the American experience when he concluded that . . . 'all men are created equal'" and that they are endowed . . . with certain "inalienable" rights.[34]

As Parrington so aptly puts it, "It is not true to say that Jefferson was reciting Locke with modifications derived from French humanists. It is nearer to the truth to say that he made use of old-world philosophy to express and justify certain tendencies then seeking adequate statement."[35] When Jefferson wrote of "life, liberty and the pursuit of happiness," he was simply giving voice to the American Dream.

The United States Constitution. Despite the revolutionary idealism that inspired American patriots during the War for Independence, it must be remembered that beginning with Jamestown and Plymouth, there were two sides to the American Dream: an idealistic side and a materialistic side. While the former represented high-minded, romantic concepts of liberty and democracy, the latter remained unshakably pragmatic, representing real-world, practical concepts of security and property. American history is a record of the struggle between these two sides of the national dream. The Declaration of Independence championed the rights of man and the idealistic side of the dream, while the United States Constitution championed the rights of property and the materialistic side of the American Dream. In the beginning, one dream tempered the other.

When the fighting was over, the new nation began operations under the 1777 Articles of Confederation, establishing a weak central governmental organization that in most matters yielded to the sovereignty of the individual states. Meanwhile all of the states drafted constitutions of their own, drawing on precepts of English law including the right to due process and to speedy trail by a jury of one's peers as well as bans on self-incrimination, standing armies, excessive bail, and cruel and unusual punishment. Most placed the army under civilian control, and many included new uniquely American provisions like freedom of the press, expanded religious freedom, and broader assurances of free speech and assembly. Still, the Articles of Confederation had created a toothless central authority, and it was becoming increasingly clear that America needed a strong and well-crafted central government to hold things together and to secure both liberty and property.[36]

By the time the Congress met to consider a new constitution in 1787, a remarkable change had taken place. The framers of the Constitution, many of whom had sung the lofty songs of revolutionary idealism before and during the war, forsook the liberal melodies that had served them so well in the fight with England. They set aside the idea of natural rights and romantic interpretations of politics and turned realist.[37] Once the English tyrant had been defeated and liberty seemingly attained, the material side of the American Dream quickly re-asserted itself and won dominion over the new nation's once-soaring idealistic aspirations. French humanitarian concepts of equality and fraternity found little response in an America, again worshipping at the altar of economic individualism.

The character of Alexander Hamilton stood at the center of America's early materialistic preoccupation. Parrington points to "his absorbing interest in the rising system of credit and finance" and his "his cool unconcern for the social consequences of his policies." "That power which holds the purse-strings absolutely, must rule," he stated without equivocation. In this climate, the architects of the American Constitution sought to create a government that would maintain a stable balance among the economic interests of the various classes. "The revolutionary concept of equalitarianism, that asserted the rights of man apart from property and superior to property, did not enter into their thinking."[38]

At the core of this shift in focus lay a great cynicism, which was most eloquently and convincingly voiced by Alexander Hamilton. Like all cynics, Hamilton lacked faith in human nature. For the common people he had only contempt, as expressed in his alleged notorious comment, "The people! The people is a great beast."[39] Like many of the founding fathers, Hamilton believed that too much democracy led to mob rule by a "tyrannical majority," intent upon destroying property rights.[40] Like many of his fellow delegates, he found it "unthinkable that government should not reflect the wishes of property."[41] He argued in favor of a powerful chief executive, elected for life. He even suggested that the office be made hereditary.[42] Concerning the structure of legislature, he wrote, "Nothing but a permanent body can check the imprudence of democracy."[43]

On the other side of the constitutional debate were the followers of Thomas Jefferson, who believed that men were fundamentally good and that they could and would rise to the callings of a democratic government, if it were structured in a prudent and responsible way. For Jefferson, democracy was the ultimate form of political organization and the end to which the Revolution and the American experiment was dedicated.[44]

Commanding the middle ground in the great constitutional debate was the majority, led by John Adams. By 1787 this group had tempered their former revolutionary idealism with a healthy dose of materialistic realism. They sought a liberal, republican, representative government, but like Hamilton, they subscribed to the cynicism of the age: they mistrusted human nature. Adams stated this mistrust outright when he wrote, "all men are bad by nature. . . ."[45] In mistrusting human nature, he mistrusted the majority, and thus he feared democracy. In Adams' own words, "Democracy never lasts long. It soon wastes, exhausts, and murders itself. There never was a democracy that did not commit suicide."[46] Adams was thus wary of the American Dream's idealistic side. He referred to the ideas disseminated by propagandists like Thomas Paine and theorists like Jefferson as the "mischief of romantic dreams." What the country needed, he thought, was a good dose of realism to bring patriotic heads down out of the clouds. But unlike Hamilton, Adams and his realistic followers sought to check "the aggressions of the rich as much as the turbulence of the poor."[47] So it was that they proposed a middle ground: a government built around a series of checks and balances. And so it was to be.

The majority of Americans strongly differed with the founding fathers when it came to defining what was meant by the "sovereignty of the people," and initially the Constitution met with widespread disfavor. After so much idealistic, revolutionary zeal, the new federal government was a disappointment for many. Most were uncomfortable with the transfer of power away from the states. Rank and file citizens were afraid of a powerful central government defined by this "backroom instrument" prepared by "aristocrats and moneyed men." In the backcountry, lingering memories of pre-revolutionary squabbles with the ruling colonial elite on the coast revived old cynicism. The majority view of the new constitution was expressed by men like Amos Singletary of Sutton, Massachusetts, who wrote, "These lawyers and men of learning and moneyed men, that talk so finely and gloss over matters so smoothly, to make poor illiterate people swallow down the pill, expect to get the Constitution for themselves; they expect to be the managers of the Constitution, and get all the power and the money into their own hands. . . . "[48] Thus Hamiltonian cynicism at the top begot popular cynicism at the bottom.

Nonetheless, Hamilton and the Federalists quickly took up the business of government with confidence. But with the coming of the French Revolution and the lofty ideals it proclaimed, a new spirit of idealism began to rise in America. The vast majority of Americans, who were still numbered among the politically disinherited, were aroused to a new political consciousness.[49] Dissatisfaction with the cynicism of federalism was mounting fast, and the idealistic side of the American Dream was about to re-assert itself. Jefferson, the consummate politician, was waiting in the wings, and with his election to the presidency in 1800, it appeared the tide had at last turned, and that the dream of liberty would at last scribe a new high-water mark.

As Thomas Jefferson was sworn in, he could not have known that the material side of the American Dream was gathering its forces for counterattack. This time its armies would advance under the new, nineteenth-century banners of modern capitalism and the industrial revolution.

5

The Two Faces of the American Dream, 1800–1865

The differences between the visions of Hamilton and Jefferson clearly illustrate the differences between the two faces of the American Dream. The harsh, conservative material realism of Hamilton, with its unbending defense of property stands out clearly against the backdrop of the libertarian idealism of Jefferson. In a similar fashion, Jefferson's reliance on a nation of farmers to champion the new nation's dreams of personal liberty today appears naïve indeed when put to the test of Hamiltonian economic practicality. Nonetheless with Jefferson's inauguration in 1800, it seemed that the idealistic side of the dream had gained the upper hand. But few envisioned the sweeping changes that the new century would bring. American capitalism, with its elastic credit, grasping speculation, and dehumanizing industrialization was just beyond the horizon, and Jeffersonian liberals were blind to its implications. The material side of the American Dream was busy preparing a new vision of American life wholly unlike the pastoral agrarian dreams of Thomas Jefferson. A new American middle class was about to thrust aside "gentleman and farmer alike, and refashion America after its own ideal."[1] For Jefferson and his followers, the price of this new American Dream would seem very high.

The Virginia Dynasty, 1800–1828
Jefferson's power lay in the fact that he appealed to America's idealism and simplicity. In Virginia supporters like John Randolph heralded the Jefferson administration as "the full

tide of successful experiment" in which "public confidence abounded."[2] But in the north cynical dissenters like Fisher Ames voiced fears that America had become "too big for union, too sordid for patriotism and too democratic for liberty,"[3] while New England church leaders warned that Jefferson's victory meant "terror, atheism and free love."[4]

Indeed Jefferson's original vision of democracy was simple. For him the success of democracy revolved around the moral strength of the nation's small independent yeoman farmers, who knew little class distinction and placed little emphasis on commerce or industry.[5] But as Jefferson took his oath, commerce and industry were abroad in the land, and the economic changes of the early years of the new century soon threatened his dream of an agricultural utopia. Ever the consummate politician, Jefferson was more sensitive to national trends and needs than he was to ideas for their own sake, and so he would slowly modify his views regarding America's industrial stirrings. Later his followers and fellow Virginians, Madison and Monroe, were forced to "beat a faltering and unmistakable retreat from original Jeffersonian positions."[6]

By the end of the Virginia Dynasty in the 1820s, economic changes in America had shattered the Arcadian dreams of Jefferson and his followers. Driven by these changes, regional differences became more pronounced. The East was discovering an industrial capitalistic order of great cities and social readjustment; the South was reveling in the prosperity gained from cotton, sparked by new demand in the North, while slavery was becoming more and more entrenched as an economic necessity; and finally, in the West, the trend was decentralizing, idealistic, and middle class in spirit, exalting in land speculation and exploitation of abundant resources. Everywhere human selfishness seemed to be distorting civil conduct.[7]

The new industrialism had to be reckoned with. "Banks, mills, factories, capital, industrial labor . . . were all distasteful realities for orthodox Jeffersonians."[8] Acceptance of the unpropertied classes involved a great retreat for the Virginians, and toward the end of his life Jefferson would almost cynically despair, "When we get piled up upon each other in large cities, as in Europe, we shall become corrupt, as in Europe, and go to eating one another as they do there."[9] At the end of the reign of the Virginia Dynasty "the gap between government and nation was a gap between minds still bound up with land on the one hand . . . and rising industries in the North on the other. It was most deeply an intellectual gap. The trading past of the eighteenth century was done; and its place was taken not simply by different ways of making money, but by a different outlook on all nature,"[10] and by different dreams.

The Industrial Revolution in America

When Thomas Jefferson became president in 1800, America was a nation of farmers. More than half a century later, when the last of the Jacksonian presidents left office and the Civil War began, America was still a nation of farmers. But as the new century unfolded, strong winds of change began to blow in the North. The change was not rapid; in fact the Industrial Revolution was more like an insidious evolution than a glorious revolution. It began with the division of labor. Then came centralization into factories, and later, with the addition of capital, came mechanization. Along the way, great cities rose, and a new American way of life was born.

With all of this came a gradual refashioning of the material side of the American Dream. No longer just a simple vision of thrift and land, hard work and self-sufficiency, the new dream was to become more complex and more powerful than the old, and it would promise much more. At the same time, it would prove more fickle, more capricious, more prone to disappoint. In the end it was a devil's bargain, for the price of the new material side of the American Dream was a ration of that precious individualism that had sustained all of America's dreams from the very beginning.

The Industrial Revolution came late to America, but by 1820 it had begun to put down roots in the northeast. This budding regional phenomenon was set against a national backdrop of westward migration, territorial expansion, and escalating immigration. Jefferson acquired the vast American heartland west of the Mississippi River in 1803, and by the time of the Civil War, the U.S. had increased its territory by another 50 percent by adding Texas, California, Oregon, and Florida. At the same time the nation's population had grown from 2.5 million at the time of the revolution to a staggering 31.5 million by 1860 while the number of states had increased from 13 to 33.

During this period there appeared on the scene a new breed of American dreamer, whose imaginative gift for mechanized invention and organization propelled not only the engines of America's fledgling industry but those of her agriculture and transportation as well. From all over Europe, new immigrants flowed into this great mixing pot of dreamlike visions and nightmarelike inventions. Most sought to avail themselves of the fruit of the old agrarian American Dream, but new factories beckoned and so did the great cities that sprang up around them. Between 1820 and 1850 the combined population of New York, Philadelphia, Boston, and Baltimore rose from 343,000 to 1,162,000, and by 1840, the urban movement was larger than the westward migration.[11] The Industrial Revolution had arrived in America, and with it came a new kind of American Dream.

The new dream was material to the core, and it promised enormous wealth. Here was Horatio Alger's "rags to riches" dream, an optimistic but grasping and crassly material vision of American business and industry fabricated in the late nineteenth century and twisted into a metaphor for economic success in the 1930s and 1940s. The new industrial myth rewarded more than just hard work; it put great store in entrepreneurial spirit, risk-taking, moxie, ruthlessness, and cunning. But in reality the upward mobility it promised proved unlikely. Fewer than five out of one hundred wealthy Americans had started out poor.[12] For those that did not make the grade, the outlook was often dreary indeed. As Henry David Thoreau saw it, workers in the new urban factories "lived in quiet desperation, sick at heart, their integrity menaced, clouded and compromised."[13]

In the beginning, American business had cynically presented itself as the champion of liberty and the savior of the American Dream of democracy. Business leaders boasted that they had overturned the power of land and thus brought down the old aristocracy. But it was not long before they showed their true colors. They too sought power above all else; American business would become just another master.[14]

The machine age had changed the American Dream forever. The old dream of freedom and democracy would linger, but the new material dream of personal wealth apart from the land had exacted an exorbitant price in the East. In the beginning it appeared to be a recipe for cynicism, a fool's wager in which one risked a life of hopeless drudgery against the dim prospect of material wealth. But as the years went by it was to become much, much more.

Adam Smith and the American Dream

The new capitalistic American Dream would be built on intellectual foundations laid out by an Englishman, Adam Smith. Smith published his famous *Inquiry into the Nature and Causes of the Wealth of Nations* in 1776. It was widely read in the United States, and the founding fathers employed many of Smith's ideas in creating an economic system to support their new American experiment. Indeed, Smith himself believed that, among the nations of the world, America was best pursuing his prescribed course to wealth, and this observation was the basis of his accurate predictions of America's future greatness.[15]

For the most part, the doctrines expounded in *The Wealth of Nations* were not original to Adam Smith. They came from Hume and Locke, as well as from the French school: Quesnay and Montesquieu and Voltaire and Rousseau. Smith's contribution was to take all of this uncoordinated speculation and arrange it into a coherent theorem of economic science, which he was careful to set within the context of history.[16] His long, daunting work dealt with price theory, wage theory, rent theory, and the roles of capital, labor, and land in creating wealth.

Central to Smith's work was the idea that wealth springs from labor, and he was the first to contemplate the efficiency inherent in division of labor. At the very core of all his ideas lay the concept that men, when free to pursue their own economic ends, will inadvertently create what is best for society as a whole. Smith believed that the combination of God's benevolence and the natural liberty of every man to pursue his self-interest combined to form what he called an "invisible hand," which acted on behalf of the well-being of society. Smith therefore concluded that economic utopia could be achieved only if both workers and manufacturers were free to pursue their own best advantage unfettered by government. This is the core of Adam Smith's famous *laissez faire* (let it be) theory of economics.

There was much here for Americans to love. First, the emphasis on labor as the key to the creation of wealth played right into American individualism, self-worth, and self-reliance, upon which all the dreams of the new nation had been erected. Second, the thinking behind Smith's *laissez faire* theory came from the same sources as the "natural rights" theories that had been so influential at the time of the revolution.

In fact, despite their seemingly opposing views Hamilton,

Jefferson, and Jackson all found something to love in Adam Smith. Even though Smith's work formed a scathing indictment of almost everything Hamilton held dear, he found Smith's notions regarding manufacturing and the division of labor compelling. On the other side of the debate, Jefferson embraced Smith on purely idealistic grounds. Applauding *laissez faire* theory with its libertarian underpinnings, he found that it neatly justified his efforts to import manufactured goods from Europe in order to keep America a nation of farmers. Jefferson wrote that he considered *The Wealth of Nations* to be "the best book extant" on economic questions.[17] Nonetheless, Jefferson would never accept Smith's theories regarding the place of labor over land in the wealth equation, nor was there much room for manufacturing in Jefferson's original utopian views.

Jackson was undoubtedly the most faithful of Smith's believers, for he counted both agricultural workers and factory laborers among his supporters in his battle to broaden the political base in America. Smith's classic argument against monopoly strongly appealed to Jacksonians, as did his views on currency, his labor theory of value and his distinction between productive and unproductive labor.[18] In 1838, the champion of the laboring class, Theodore Sedgewick, would observe that Adam Smith's "voice has been ringing in the world's ears for over sixty years, but it is only now in the United States he is listened to, reverenced and followed."[19]

Adam Smith failed to foresee the enormous changes that the industrial revolution would bring. But he was aware of the dark shadows his division of labor theory cast upon the future lives of the working classes. The great economist knew that if one treated labor as a commodity to be bought and sold, a very inhuman civilization would result.[20] Perhaps Hamilton realized this as well, but he cared little for the masses; Jefferson never envisioned real industrialization getting off the ground in America; and so it was left to Andrew Jackson to face the challenges of the Industrial Revolution in America.

As Jackson took up the gauntlet, the words of Adam Smith must have been ringing his ears. "Those exertions of the natural liberty of a few individuals, which might endanger the security of the whole society . . . ought to be restrained by the laws of all governments. . . . "[21] Thinking along the same lines, Fenimore Cooper summed up the Jacksonian position, "Commerce is entitled to a complete and efficient protection in all of its legal rights, but the moment it presumes to control . . . it should be frowned on and rebuked."[22] Jackson's aim was not to stifle free commerce, but to safeguard the equitable distribution of property, which he felt alone could sustain democracy. He began by attempting to break the banking monopoly by enacting general laws of incorporation, and then applied the same kind of reform to the entire corporate system.[23] Thus, with the *Wealth of Nations* as his bible, Jackson and his followers brought the full force of the federal government to bear against the rising menace of corporate abuse, and in the process yet another fragile Arcadian flower of Jefferson's idyllic American Dream was trampled underfoot. Jefferson had agreed with Thomas Paine when he said, "That government is best which governs least." Jackson may have wanted to agree, but he was compelled by circumstance to do otherwise.

The Age of Jackson, 1828–1860

When the last of the Virginia presidents, John Quincy Adams, moved into the White House in 1824, working men and small farmers everywhere were cynical, thinking that he represented "the betrayal of the Jeffersonian promise of equal rights in favor of special benefits for a single class."[24] It appeared that the material side of the American Dream was again gaining the upper hand, and that the rout of Jeffersonian idealism was complete. Four years later, the great populist Andrew Jackson opened his political arms to the western farmers and the property-less masses in the east. In so doing he revived the Jeffersonian dream in America.

Jacksonian democracy represented "a second American phase of that enduring struggle between the business community and the rest of society...,"[25] that is to say between the idealistic and the material sides of the American Dream. Jackson understood that America had changed, and its Dream with it. He knew that new approaches would be required to keep the fires of liberty burning amid the smoke of industry. Like Jefferson, Jackson believed that property should be held subordinate to the rights of individuals. The specific problem was to control capitalism for the benefit of the common man. In order to accomplish this Jackson and his followers "moderated the side of Jeffersonianism that talked of agricultural virtue, ... natural property and abolition of industrialism and expanded immensely the side which talked of economic equality, human rights and control of industrialism. This readjustment enabled the Jacksonians to attack economic problems that had baffled and defeated the Jeffersonians."[26]

Many view the age of Jackson as an era of populism and so-called "coonskin democracy." Indeed, for decades after Jackson's election, it seemed only a man born in a log cabin could capture the American presidency. But Jacksonian democracy was about a great deal more than log cabins. It reharnessed the idealist side of the American Dream, which had fled Virginia to the vast expanses of the American West and then swept back eastward on the coattails of Old Hickory himself, only to migrate once more to New England where the newly employed working masses had welcomed it with open arms. Andrew Jackson understood what the French traveler, Alexis de Tocqueville, meant when he wrote in his insightful 1835 *Democracy in America*, " ... democracy thrives only if it sees to the universal distribution of hope."[27] Andrew

Jackson understood the importance of hope because Andrew Jackson understood the American Dream.

The American Renaissance

The problem with The American Dream of democracy in the Age of Jackson was that, despite the Jacksonians' best efforts, it mutated into myriad regional political and economic interpretations that were far from uniform. In the industrial North democracy meant one thing, in the agrarian South another, and in the decentralized West yet another. In the process, the concept of service to a common well-being had been lost beyond all recovery.[28] A new kind of dreamer was needed to gather up the scattered fabric of America's hope and sew it back into a single serviceable garment that fit all.

To answer this call came the first wave of important American writers. The American Renaissance was an unprecedented literary outpouring of American idealism led by the New England Transcendentalists, whose spokesmen, Emerson, and hero, Thoreau, and poet, Whitman, would affirm the beauty of a renewed American Dream of human perfectibility and perfect democracy, while the skeptic, Hawthorne, and the pessimist, Melville, would warn the young nation of the dangers inherent in false dreams.[29] In their unswerving idealism, all would become unflinching critics of an America badly in need of criticism. The old American Dream with all of its fragmented manifestations was again on the brink of crisis. The growing nation had reached "that great watershed in the life of modern societies" when economic forces expand and become dominant.[30] The material side of the American Dream was once again being overpowered by the idealistic side.

Transcendentalism was an assertion of the essential worth of man and the divinity of human instinct. It was the last flaring up of the old equalitarian idealism that was being threatened by new scientific and materialistic dreams.[31] Just as de Tocqueville had predicted, the ideals of equality and free-dom were in conflict, a conflict made especially vigorous when freedom's cause was material. The idealism of Emerson and Thoreau was so great that they were constantly impatient with and disappointed by, an America given over to materialism. For lesser men this would have been a formula for cynicism, and in the impassioned fire of their criticism, they often tee-tered near the brink.

Emerson's loss of faith during the 1850s is clear. Al-though he still believed in man's perfectibility, he saw human nature as easily duped and led astray. "Shall we judge this coun-try by the majority or the minority?" He would ask. "Certainly the minority," he would conclude, and then sounding for all the world like a latter day Alexander Hamilton, he would add, "The mass are animal . . . near the chimpanzee." He even went so far as to lament the outcome of the Revolutionary War on the grounds that if England had won, the slaves would have been freed in 1833. Most of all, Emerson saw clearly the "dan-gers of commerce." "This invasion of nature by trade with its money, its credit, its steam, its railroad, threaten to upset the balance of man and establish a new universal monarchy more tyrannical than . . . Rome," he ranted in his journal. Exclama-tions like, "Human nature is as bad as it can be," and "If it were possible to repair the rottenness of human nature . . . it were well," sparked Vernon Parrington to remark that, "at times he seems half persuaded . . . that the potential children of light are 'strangely and fiercely possessed of the Devil.'"[32] "Man is not what man should be," Emerson wrote, "He is a treadle on a wheel. He is a tassel at the apron string of society. He is a chest of money."[33] For Ralph Waldo Emerson, there could be no true democracy until the material world was subordi-nated to a higher value, until the idealistic side of the Ameri-can Dream reassumed its rightful place above its materialistic other half.

Henry David Thoreau was an equally stern judge, and he too held his age in low esteem. In his famous *On the Duty of Civil Disobedience,* he wrote that he agreed with Thomas Paine "that government is best, which governs least." He would then sum up his true belief in a sarcastic quip: "That government is best, which governs not at all."[34] After his experience at Walden Pond, Thoreau had a vision of an America come face to face with "the enemies of the moral life: the new industrialism, which would deform it, and the government, which would corrupt it."[35] There is often only a fine line between the involved critic and the detached cynic. "Beware of all enterprises that require new clothes," Thoreau warns us, presumably with a straight face.

As to the great novelists of the American Renaissance, two tower above the rest: Nathaniel Hawthorne and Herman Melville. Each viewed the America of the mid-nineteenth century with a critical eye. Hawthorne mistrusted the Transcendentalist vision of the divine instinct of man. Man to him seemed "as likely to be the child of the Devil as the first born of God." His recurrent theme is the examination of evil "which forever waylays human life and . . . brings havoc to our hopes."[36] Hester Prynne's story of heroic freedom ending in moral anarchy is illustrative of this theme.[37] And so is Hawthorne's *Celestial Railroad,* a satire in which a railroad journey represents an illusory voyage to salvation. As it turns out, the same train can take us to hell.[38] As for Melville, we need only consider Ahab, whose "fanatical dream suggests both heroism and tragic delusion."[39]

The Transcendentalists of the American Renaissance celebrated the American Dream with visions of self-reliance, limitless potential, and perfect democracy. Sadly, in their real-life examinations they discovered that "freedom seemed to lead to anarchy and democracy to despair,"[40] and in the end, they were unable to repair the idealistic side of the American

Dream. The material side of the dream was too powerful, too alluring, and too entrenched even for America's greatest men of letters. In this case the pen would not prove mightier than the sword, nor did it appear more powerful than the almighty dollar.

The American Civil War

A house divided against itself could not stand, and neither could a dream. Under the pressure of the American love affair with the machine, the American Dream began to splinter. Along with new factories came new roads and canals and steamboats and railroads probing into a once pastoral wilderness. It was the beginning of a new phase of the material side of the American Dream: the dream of progress.[41] Here was a dynamic eastern dream of change and control that was not fully comprehended by its dreamers, to say nothing of a nation of farmers. In the South a different dream was evolving. It was marked by the resurgence of an aristocratic ideal that frankly recognized local economic interests.[42] As these diverse regional dreams materialized and took shape, the national dream of union dissolved. The issue finally came down to slavery, an issue that split the nation not only geographically between north and south, but also economically between industrial and agrarian and ideologically between states rights and union.[43]

Thus the lost dreams carried down in defeat were about more than just slavery. Also carried down were "the old ideals of decentralized democracy and of individual liberty, and with the overthrow of these traditional principles in their last refuge, the nation hurried along the path of an unquestioning and uncritical consolidation that was to throw the coercive power of a centralizing state into the hands of the new industrialists."[44] After the war, the American Dream of democracy came to be interpreted by the rising captains of industry as the right to use the government of the all people for the benefit of the few. Out of the smoke of the great battle, the material side of the American Dream emerged victorious. But it was not in full control.

6

The Plunder of the American Dream, 1865–1929

Rising out of the carnage of civil war a new American Dream loomed above the landscape unlike anything that had gone before: greedy, capable, ambitious, ruthless. The machine was loose in the garden, and it stood on the threshold of a continental expansion that would transfer sovereignty from the dying heirs of Jacksonian democracy to the newly made captains of industry. With the agrarian idealism of the South destroyed, only the scattered democratic faith of the farmers of the Middle Border and the individualistic pioneers of the western frontier stood in its way.

American industry had flourished during the war in the North, consolidating, amassing capital, refining its technological potential, and preparing for further conquests. With the idealistic watch-dogs of the Constitution in disarray, its trend gained momentum and power, and it thrust westward, gathering to its bosom a mushrooming population, powerful new technologies, abundant natural resources, and increasingly liquid capital. "The machine would reach the remotest villages to disrupt the traditional domestic economy, and the division of labor would substitute for the versatile frontiersmen the specialized factory hand."[1] Almost overnight, a nation of farmers was being transformed into a nation of workers; a rural agricultural people were far too quickly becoming an urbanized industrial people: rootless, colorless, homogeneous. The thoughtful individualism that had supported the idealistic side of the American Dream since the very beginning was being destroyed, and a ruthless, grasping individualism was loose on the land creating a new, grotesquely materialistic American Dream.

The Gilded Age

This new materialistic American Dream aspired to a new kind of progress, and it thrived in the postwar era Mark Twain called the Gilded Age. After the war, the idealistic side of the American Dream had been put carelessly away without regard for the future of liberty, democracy, or the common good while Americans eagerly applied themselves to the business of acquiring money. Here was a reckless new dream out of control, propelling change at a rate so rapid as to outstrip conventional institutions and philosophies; a cynical dream, grasping and unlovely, which, under the banner of *laissez faire,* paid unctuous lip service to the old idealistic American Dream of liberty and democracy, while shamelessly attempting to shatter all bonds of democratic control. Even Walt Whitman, the hopeful, undisputed poet laureate of American democracy, would despair: "Democracy grows rankly up the thickest, noxious, deadliest plants of all—brings worse and worse invaders—needs newer, larger, stronger, keener, compensations and compellers."[2]

In the currency of the Gilded Age, the new American Dream of progress was measured by more growth, more wealth, more land, more exploitation, more technology, more power. For immigrants it was more than a dream of wealth and progress, it was a dream of new beginning; and they poured in from all over Europe until, in the first decade of the new century, the inflow exceeded one million annually.[3] The national population went from 35 million at the end of the Civil war to 60 million in 1890 and nearly 100 million in 1914.[4] Great cities mushroomed up out of the prairie. Factories appeared everywhere. Steel rails banded the nation together. Exploitation of natural resources proceeded in a similarly reckless orgy: coal, steel, fisheries, grazing land, timber, mechanized agriculture, precious metals. The wealth of America was being harvested without regard to consequence, all in the name of the new Dream of Progress, while elected officials stood by with their hands deep in the till.

The Gilded Age and its new American Dream of progress were the results of past decades of thrift and want, the product of a nation too long deprived. Americans had had enough of the narrow poverty of frontier life. As the frontier disappeared, frontier individualism was quickly "simplified into an acquisitive instinct," and there followed a vigorous, undisciplined age of waning ethical values. As Vernon Parrington describes them, these new Americans dreamers "were primitive souls, ruthless, predatory, capable, single-minded men, rogues and rascals often, but never feeble, never hindered by petty scruples, never given to puling or whining—the raw materials for a race of capitalistic buccaneers."[5] The most American of all of America's Dreams begot the most American epic in our nation's history. But there would be a heavy price to pay.

The End of the Frontier

All the while the frontier was disappearing. In 1860 the population of Kansas was about 100,000; in 1890, the year the frontier was officially (and perhaps prematurely) declared no longer to exist, Kansas boasted almost a million and a half inhabitants. It may appear paradoxical, but the same kind of frontier individualism that had given birth to the reckless, grasping, unfettered materialism of the Gilded Age fostered the idealistic crusade that would later endeavor to bring this orgy of capitalistic excess under control. The two sides of the American Dream were again about to do battle.[6]

Throughout the Gilded Age the frontier had beckoned to the faceless masses that had been conscripted into industrialism's numbing regiment. Just as the siren call of the virgin North American continent had once lured European dreamers, free land in the West had projected similar visions of escape and new beginning to laborers trapped in the slums of the great cities of the East. For these hapless cogs in the wheel, the western frontier appeared to be a democratic Eden, untainted by the machine—a place that still dreamed the old idealistic American Dreams of liberty and democracy, of economic equality and freedom to rise.[7] But as the frontier shrank, those immigrants and westerners who had lost in the great gambles of the Gilded Age were added to the growing ranks of the proletariat. The rich became richer and more cynical in their manipulations of government and power. The poor became poorer and more cynical in their disillusionment and helplessness. In the end, the frontier would be gone, and western American society would soon mirror industrialized eastern American society with its standardization and machine culture. The primitive frontier conditions that had nurtured individualism and faith in the idealistic side of American Dream would disappear with the frontier. Nonetheless, the idealistic side of the dream would live on in the West to become the platform for future assaults on the plundering material side of the American Dream of progress. The idealistic side of the American Dream would again rise in the West, and it would soon seek to "complete the work begun by Jacksonian democracy and attempt to create political machinery that would enable democracy to withstand the shock of the Industrial Revolution."[8]

The Beginnings of Criticism

Sadly, the rebuilding of Jacksonian ideals would prove an impossible dream when opposed by pervasive and ambitious Gilded Age industrialism and its ruthless leaders who were openly and quite cynically buying and selling the political state.

As the plunder of the new material side of the American Dream continued, thoughtful Americans were losing faith. The old heroes of the Enlightenment were suddenly impotent, and the manipulative new heroes of reckless materialism were demagogues: selfish, corrupt, and mired in unlovely public scandals of all sorts. To have come to this after a hundred years was unthinkable. Skepticism and cynicism had been on the rise since the 1850s, and finally in the 1890s, they burst into brief but billowing flames crackling with a new kind of criticism. Only flickering at first, the new criticism was initially brushed aside by the overpowering material lust of the age. Nonetheless its smoldering embers remained to later ignite a totally different kind of American Dream.

Cynical Voices. America had failed to see what was before its very eyes. Unlike Europe, in the last decades of the nineteenth century the nation had produced no great critics of industrialism—no Carlyle, no Ruskin, and no great social critics like Marx and Engels. Walt Whitman, who belonged to the earlier age, was perhaps the only exception. But by 1890 the aging poet and fearless critic of American democracy was dying in despair, leaving only Mark Twain, an authentic American child of the frontier, to carry the torch. This buoyant humorist of the 1870s would become the bitter satirist of the 1890s. "If you pick up a starving dog and make him prosperous, he will not bite you. This is the principal difference between a dog and a man,"[9] he would cynically quip in 1894. But the aging Mr. Clements was not all jest. Twain's late work also manifests, "the fierce satire of disillusionment, the cry of the idealist who realizes at last how greatly he has been cheated by his dreams."[10] This assessment is clearly affirmed by Twain's own words, ". . . the human spirit cannot long watch with indifference the remotely human caravan hastening to eternity—cannot find food for laughter alone in the incredible meanness and folly of men cheating and quarreling in a wilderness of graves." Later he turned to pure cynicism, "The human race consists of the damned and the ought-to-be damned."[11] Or "Every human is pathetic. The secret source of humor itself is not joy but sorrow."[12] And finally there is Mark Twain on the American Dream, ". . . frankly and inherently insane—like all dreams . . . the silly creations of an imagination that is not conscious of its freaks. . . ." As Vernon Parrington so neatly puts it, "The Mysterious Stranger is only Tom Sawyer in the midnight of disillusion."[13]

Along with Mark Twain's later work, the novels of Stephen Crane, Frank Norris, and Theodore Dreiser reflect the bitter disillusionment of America in the 1890s. Beyond the work of these few and the poems of Emily Dickinson, the literature of Gilded Age was a poor rejoinder to the clarion call of the American Renaissance of the former generation. Christened "The Brown Decades" by critic Lewis Munford, the age "shook down the blossoms of promise" that had been nurtured by Emerson, Whitman, and Thoreau and "blasted the promise of spring."[14]

Science and the American Dream. A great deal more than war and crude material plunder were to "blast" America's Emersonian "blossoms of promise." After the Civil War the new scientific spirit that lay at the very root of the Industrial Revolution slowly began to alter old patterns of thought.

Charles Darwin's *Origin of the Species* had been published in 1859, and the social, political, and economic implications of Darwin's theory were ready-made grist for Gilded Age capitalists and their greedy mills. Embracing the ideas of so-called Social Darwinism, cynical industrialists quickly wrapped themselves in the new philosophy of human fulfillment put forward by the Englishman Herbert Spencer. Spencer insisted that, when free to exercise their natural rights, individuals would naturally realize their full potential; but he also insisted that no matter how brutal the process, the state must not interfere.[15] It was a simple, self-regulating *laissez faire* version of "the survival of the fittest," and for many it confirmed the American experience.[16] This concept appealed not only to the upwardly mobile and the captains of industry, but also to the waves of immigrants that were pouring in. Driven hard and often exploited as workers, they clung tenaciously to their dreams of a better life.[17]

But as the Gilded Age wore on, widespread realizations of this vision of self-rewarding freedom failed to materialize. The poor were not fulfilled. They were only becoming poorer. Something was terribly wrong with a progress that augmented poverty as it increased wealth. The individual was being dwarfed by poverty, monotony, and drab standardization.

Indeed, American individualism was being dwarfed by a great deal more than the social and economic forces of run-away industrialism. Gone with the Enlightenment were the comforting, optimistic, humanizing visions of Locke and Rousseau. In their place was the cold empiricism of science. The irony was that the material gifts of the new industrialism had been part of the American Dream since the 1830s, but the vibrant self-reliance upon which the dream rested soon fell prey to the very science that had created the industrial age in the first place. A new technological revolution was pushing back the "boundaries of space and time," reorienting "the mind toward all ultimate problems" and bringing "into question all traditional faiths, political and social, as well as theological and philosophical." This darkly cynical force not only threatened individualism and personal fulfillment; it lapped at the very dykes of human purpose. In the great scheme of things, man had become a pinpoint, a speck, a tiny gear in a great cosmic mechanism—amoral, impersonal, interdependent "tied by a thousand invisible threads to the encompassing whole."[18]

From freedom to determinism, such had been the drift of thought that science had imposed upon the American Dream; such was the beginning of the journey that was to reshape America's view of industrial life. But the dream was not dead. It had become a chrysalis, reinventing itself. And out of an age of despair would come a revolutionary new kind of collective American Dream.

Third Party Movements. On the threshold of the twentieth century, American society, like the machines that fed it, was becoming increasingly complex. Urbanization and the dark mood of determinism fostered by the new science, along with the dehumanizing effects of the division of labor, all combined to create a growing sense of helplessness among factory workers. America's farmers were also feeling exploited and impotent in the face of blatant market manipulations by cynical capitalists. After more than a hundred years, a nation built on lusty individualism was finding that the individual working alone was powerless.

For the common man the situation was desperate. Wages tumbled; small farms failed, and the Panic of 1893 left many Americans destitute. The frontier was gone, the nation's resources had been squandered, and cynicism was growing as faith in progress, justice, democracy, and the excellence of human nature slowly waned. America's traditional political machinery was suddenly proving incompatible with reality. The Industrial Revolution was submerging the ideals of the American Revolution. For perhaps the first time in American history, serious social unrest was fermenting, and the American Dream was teetering.

With the power of the individual seemingly destroyed, workers and farmers joined together in groups to organize strikes and form alliances. Out of this collective turmoil rose powerful third party movements: the Greenback Party, the Farmer's Alliance, and finally Populism. Like so many idealists before them, their goal was to reposition the rights of man above those of property. If the individual was no longer up to the task, then a drastic assertion of the power of government was needed to put the American Dream back on its foundations. In this context it is not surprising that this first great surge of American liberalism would, as Turner puts it, "react against individualism in favor of the drastic assertion of the powers of government"[19] or in the words of Parrington "attempt to secure through the political state the freedoms that before had come from un-preempted opportunity."[20]

At the heart of the struggle were American farmers. Allied with eastern blue-collar workers, they sought to wage a great battle against Wall Street and the financial power of the East. It was to be "the last mortal struggle between capitalism and agrarianism."[21] The Populists demanded free silver, government control of communication and transportation, government co-ops for the purchase of farm produce, a graduated income tax, credit for agriculture, and broad election reforms. The eastern press cried "Socialism," and so it was. Here was a sudden and unprecedented drift toward a socialized political state.

Progressive America.
By 1900 Populism in America was dead. But its impact had been great. As the new century began, many Americans had become cynical. Many believed that big business was destroying the country, and there was a growing fear that free individuals were being rendered powerless in America's new industrial landscape.[22] It was a turning point, a seismic shift in the American Dream, and what followed was the first of many steps toward the creation of a modern welfare state.

Within a generation most of the planks in the Populist ultraliberal platform had become realities through normal party politics. The so-called Progressives—Roosevelt, Taft, and Wilson—would accept the new industrial order, but they would seek to check its excesses by placing it under government regulation. As Teddy Roosevelt put it, "Our laws have failed in enforcing the performance of duty by the man of property towards the man who works for him, by the corporation to the investor, the wage earner and the general public."[23] He viewed the federal government as "an impartial tribunal, which would adjudicate between the public good and private profit."[24] The Progressives sought to re-attach the American Dream to stable moorings. Ignoring the old foundation of individualism, they would attempt to re-erect it squarely upon the shoulders of the United States government. The American Dream would never be quite the same.

The new Progressive American Dream was revolutionary. In a total reversal of Thomas Paine's "that government is best which governs least," it sought governmental power to protect the weak and helpless, prosecute monopoly, enforce child labor laws, mandate limited working hours, police safety in the workplace, eliminate corruption in government, protect natural resources and stabilize the financial system. It was a paternalistic dream of a national government that would lead the way to an idyllic society.[25] But where were the watchdogs that would police the government? Despite the enthusiasm of liberal reformers, many Americans still feared the tyranny of big government more than the tyranny of the capitalists. They clung tenaciously to the old, ingrained dream of individualism that had by this time become an inseparable part of the American soul. And when the new Progressives failed to raise the real wages of most workers, Americans became increasingly cynical regarding political remedies.

Cynicism increased as the First World War brought an

increase in the power of government coupled with an increased cooperation between government and big business. When the smoke of battle cleared, a notable backlash occurred. Progressive ideals were tossed aside, and as the twenties began, America found itself back under the heel of *laissez faire*. The old gluttonous American Dream of progress again feasted on the land. Big business thrived, and Herbert Hoover was elected in 1928 on a platform of "rugged individualism." Although for some this kind of political rhetoric appealed to a disappearing frontier spirit and masked the shallowness of material prosperity of the twenties, others sensed that something was very wrong. On the surface it appeared that America had made positive changes: rural to urban, peasant to middle class, wilderness to countryside, ignorance to education. But beneath the thin veneer of appearance, the nation's dreams were descending a rocky path from individualism to conformity, certainty to uncertainty, faith to doubt, security to insecurity, hope to disappointment.[26]

The works of the American writers of the period document the nation's disillusionment. At a moment when a fading individualism was being touted as "the gospel of American life," H. L. Mencken, like so many American journalists before him, recognized the sham and took the offensive. As Louis Kronenberger observes, "For years culture in America had been standing still, corruption had been growing and criticism on all fronts had been paralyzed by timidity and ignorance. But the War had torn off a few masks, dislodged a few certainties, given doubt and skepticism an opening. Mencken proceeded to widen and enlarge that opening."[27] But Mencken was not a reformer, and the upshot of his criticism was to encourage a cult of withdrawal. He insisted that he could "offer no remedy"; he sought only to unveil the comedic. Like Mark Twain, H. L. Mencken slowly sank into a kind of "unredeemed cynicism." His was "the tone not of a man who did not believe, but of a man who did not want to believe."[28]

Similarly, for Sinclair Lewis, the optimistic dreams of middle class capitalism were "not so golden" as they had seemed before the war. Vernon Parrington describes Lewis's "pudgy novels" as "slashing attacks on a world that in mouthing empty shibboleths is only whistling to keep up its courage."[29] For Lewis the country was past helping. What could be expected to rise from the flimsy dreams of George Babbitt or Elmer Gantry? In a strange way F. Scott Fitzgerald's characters illustrate the same theme. "The inhabitants of West Egg live what the citizens of Zenith can only dream," and in so doing they "reveal the tawdriness of the dream."[30] This now-tawdry American Dream was about to turn to ashes.

7

The Selling of the American Dream, 1929–1970

As the third decade of the new century drew to a close, the American journey from farm to factory was almost complete, and the new grasping American capitalism was proving increasingly difficult to control. When confronted with the hard demands of the new industrial age, America's old dreams no longer appeared compatible with reality. As Max Lerner puts it, the average American had been "…alienated by the machine from his old role as independent farmer-artisan-entrepreneur. . . ."[1]

The ironic fact was that, in turn-of-the-century Progressive efforts to provide the government with the power to regulate the ravenous industrial beast, America had relinquished some of the very individualism and independence that she had employed to create the beast in the first place. With the economic calamity of the 1930s, the only solution seemed to be to relinquish still more. So why in the face of such a sacrifice-gone-wrong did America not lose faith and turn to revolution or demagoguery? The answer is clear. As systematized complexity and bureaucratic interdependency grew, America had continued to trade in her old idealistic dreams for new material ones. As Dr. Lerner so aptly puts it, "The loss of a sense of independence . . . had been replaced by a feeling of well being in the realm of consumption and living standards."[2] By the time of the great crash of 1929, working Americans had acquired middle-class values.[3]

At this point the material side of the American Dream no longer consisted of vague notions of progress, upward mobility, and success. By 1929 one could put a very detailed face on it. The new standardized American Dream had been hammered into specific, reproducible, consumable shapes by American big business, while a new kind of advertising shamelessly manipulated a conforming society. Seeking to fill the void created by the loss of individualism with material abundance, advertisers transformed the luxuries of yesterday into the necessities of today. In the presidential race of 1928 a Hoover campaign ad promised "a chicken in every pot and a car in every garage." The fact that this phrase has become an enduring national metaphor for the ongoing dream of American materialism attests to the nature and specificity of the new material American Dream.

Although the success of mechanized agriculture and the advance of the internal combustion engine (especially the motorcar) had played large roles in its creation, the new material dream incorporated a great deal more than chickens and autos. It coddled an identity crisis of the now-vast American middle-class with a mind-boggling list of products: toasters and radios, washing machines and suburban homes, public schools and new notions of job security and benefits. Along with all of this, the new dream included education to achieve the dream, enough income to afford the dream and enough leisure time to enjoy it. Even the Great Depression could not shake the nation from her firm embrace of this new homogeneous American Dream.

The Great Depression and the New Deal

"The day of enlightenment has come," Franklin Roosevelt informed the American people in his campaign of 1932. "Our government owes every man an avenue to possess himself of a portion of that plenty sufficient for his needs. . . ."[4] In this vision the government was an instrument for fulfilling the new American Dream. Roosevelt knew that what he had to sell was hope, and thus the New Deal itself was calculated to instill hope by promoting this new middle-class, material vision. To this end, Congress granted Roosevelt sweeping powers and fashioned landmark legislation designed to control banking, finance, public works, housing, education, electrification, labor, and social security.

The New Deal. Roosevelt knew that for many Americans such a revolutionary regulatory approach would be a bitter pill to swallow. Although unrestrained individualism had proved a failure, he knew that "any paternalistic system which tries to provide for security for everyone from above calls for . . . a regimentation utterly uncongenial to the spirit of our people."[5] With this concern in mind, Roosevelt's New Deal was in some ways more cautious than the Progressive's efforts of the earlier generation. Unlike Teddy Roosevelt and Woodrow Wilson, Franklin Roosevelt sought economic reform to heal the acute wounds of a failing economy and not necessarily broad social reform to address the chronic illnesses of society. Although the New Deal would later favor the interests of labor and agriculture over those of business, in the beginning some of Roosevelt's critics even accused him of being soft on big business. For some political scientists the New Deal constituted a "proto cynical exercise," characterized by "interest-group negotiation, the wheeling and dealing of elite insiders and economic technocrats whose explanations concealed the familiar pork barrel and logrolling with talk of realism, expertise, and novelty."[6] Whatever his methods, Roosevelt believed that "the American Dream could only be realized if the federal government took an active, invasive and constant role."[7] At the same time, he also sensed that Americans had begun to develop "a greater cynicism about politics."[8] "The only thing we have to fear is fear itself," he would promise in a passionate attempt to buy time for his programs and to curb mounting cynicism.

John Maynard Keynes. The Great Depression confirmed for many economists a supposed heresy that some had harbored for decades. Was it possible that Adam Smith's "invisible hand" theory was flawed? Was it possible that capitalism, operating in a free environment, did not automatically create harmony between total production and total consumption? There had never really been such a thing as a "totally free environment," so no one really knew the answer. But dared one voice the fear that Marx might have been right? Then in 1936 John Maynard Keynes arrived upon the scene, and with the publication of his *General Theory of Employment Interest and Money* he said exactly that and put an end to *laissez faire* overnight and forever. Thus another of the once-sturdy foundation blocks upon which the American Dream had been built was removed.

Keynes boldly asserted that the automatic mechanism so long believed to regulate production and consumption was flawed. He then argued for "intelligent and energetic government [fiscal] action . . . to remedy this defect in the market system."[9] In order to regulate employment, he also called for a "somewhat comprehensive socialization of investment," also controlled by government fiscal policy. This came at a time when the government had already laid the stage for intervention, and so the old capitalism was laid aside. But as the twentieth century matured, the new economic theories were often cynically used to further other agendas, and there soon appeared a wide gap between the "textbook theories" of John Maynard Keynes and real-world governmental economic policies. Keynesian theory would soon come under increased scrutiny.

Out of the powerful manipulations of the government in the market place and the sweeping governmental programs of the New Deal there arose an enduring and widespread revolutionary national feeling that the federal government was about to shoulder the ultimate responsibility for the welfare, employment, and economic security of the American people.

Great Expectations

With the outbreak of war, the powers of government were further expanded, and multiple agencies were established to coordinate the war effort. But when the fighting ended after Hiroshima, for the first time in American history, the government did not shrink after war. With the arrival of the nuclear age and the perceived communist threat, wartime governmental expansion proved permanent. Breaking with tradition, America would henceforth maintain a large military in peacetime.

Despite the Cold War and the dark specter of the nuclear age, America entered the second half of the century with her dreams soaring. After all, her armies had just won decisive victories on opposite sides of the globe, her economy continued to boom as never before and her place as the leader of the free world had been firmly established. After the war the nation would bask in the sunshine of three decades of unprecedented success. *Time* editor Henry Luce had gone so far as to declare the beginning of "The American Century." According to historian James T. Patterson, "No comparable period of United States history witnessed so much economic and civic progress. In this golden age it often seemed that there were no limits to what the United States could do both at home and abroad."[10] During this era, the American Dream would acquire unrealistic, self-righteous overtones: invincible, innocent, righter of wrongs, defender of the weak, egalitarian purveyor of liberty and justice, and generous distributor of slices of the American pie. Such grand nationalistic illusions invite grand disappointments, and grand disappointments breed cynicism.

To carry the flag of the new zealot American Dream, the nation was preparing a new generation: the biggest, richest, best educated America had ever produced. These were the baby boomers. Nourished on the manufactured, standardized inventory of the new, material American Dream and spoon-fed the pabulum of the new American educational system, they were raised mouthing the platitudes of the old, now-hollow idealistic American Dream of democracy, liberty, and hope.

As the baby boomers grew up, the standardization of the material side of the American Dream was completed. At its pinnacle was the dream of home ownership facilitated by huge government agencies providing Federal Housing Administration and Veterans Administration loans. A massive internal migration to the suburbs ensued. Between 1950 and 1970 the number of suburban homes in the United States increased from 36 million to 72 million. Along with the single family home, a laundry list of lesser material dreams were fulfilled: washing machine sales went from 1.7 to 2.6 million annually between 1950 and 1960; dryer sales would double in a two year period during the 1950s; two car families doubled between 1952 and 1958; and, perhaps most importantly, by 1967, 88 percent of American homes would have TV sets.[11]

Alongside such rampant materialism, the old idealistic American Dream still appeared alive and well. In the 1950s and 1960s, there was a widespread feeling that America would spread its brand of democracy and capitalism throughout the world. Indeed, the ideals of liberty and democracy were still given reverent lip service during this period. But with the slow erosion of individualism that had been taking place for half a century, the meanings of these terms had shifted, and their relevance was less immediate than in the previous century. At its core, the new idealistic American Dream was defined by a continued belief in hard work, and the enduring faith that, with hard work, one could still rise; that children would do better than their parents; in short, that America was still a land of opportunity. This dream rested on a widespread belief that American class structure was not rigid and on an enduring faith in economic growth, technology, and education. [12]

Things looked bright indeed, but were things really as rosy as they seemed? Certainly there were reasons for concern. Living with the bomb was proving more unnerving that anyone could have guessed, and few could overlook the inherent cynicism in "threatening violence in the service of peace."[13] The McCarthy era shook the faith of many as to the adequacy of the political system. As George Kennan wrote, "A political system and public opinion . . . that could so easily be disoriented by this sort of challenge in one epoch would be no less vulnerable to a similar one in another."[14] As the 1960s approached, there was growing concern that the West was falling behind in the "Space Race." But worst of all, American intellectuals were beginning to develop doubts about the nature, substance, and consequences of the dreams America was living.

Many of America's best minds were beginning to believe that the nation had indeed traded her unique form of individualism for a ubiquitous conformity, for so many new cars and houses in the suburbs. If so, what would the consequences be? Early in the era, American writers had begun to explore the pathos inherent in the ideas of conformity and loss of identity. Sloan Wilson's novel, *The Man in the Gray Flannel Suit* (1957) depicted the drab, soulless world of suburbia and corporate America. But almost ten years earlier, Arthur Miller's *Death of a Salesman* (1949) had offered the world a more penetrating insight into the mind of a conflicted nation struggling with the core issues of the times; a disturbing yet strangely familiar portrait of the modern dilemma. Willy Loman's worn-out dreams were no longer viable. How was America to reconcile the dreams of the past with the disillusionment of the present?

In the 1950s buzzwords began to fly about as Americans were warned about "alienation," "identity crises," "the age of anxiety," "uprootedness," and the "mass society." According to David Reisman in his 1950 study *The Lonely Crowd,* the individualistic "inner-direction" of the past was giving way to a new, collective, group driven "outer-direction."[15] Six years later, William H. Whyte Jr. published *The Organization Man.* Dr. Whyte heard Americans mouthing the American Dream with its familiar insistence that the "pursuit of individual salvation through hard work, thrift and competitive struggle is at the heart of the American achievement." But he warned that the harsh facts of what he called "the organization life" did not "jibe with these precepts." Americans, Whyte said, were in denial, unable to face the fact that the old, outmoded, individualistic "Protestant Ethic" was being replaced by a new, collective "Social Ethic," which relied on sublimation to the group for personal fulfillment. Unfortunately, according to Dr. Whyte, the new "Social Ethic" was historically unworkable, "essentially a Utopian faith," an impossible attempt to merge the goals of the individual with those of the organization.[16] Perhaps the intellectuals of the era overstated the case. But whatever may have been wrong with the idealistic side of the American Dream, it was lost in the shadow of the mind-boggling abundance of the material side of the dream.

Then, out of the late 1950s, riding on this wave of optimism came John Fitzgerald Kennedy, a new kind of leader for a new kind of generation. Self-assured, confident, charming, even good-looking, he would promise the nation a New Frontier to replace the old. Marching at the head of a youthful army of baby boomers, he would lead America on a great crusade to rid the nation of social ills.

Since the early 1950s the courts had been enlarging the scope of American rights. The enforcement of new rights required new regulators, and that meant an increase in the size of government. But this was a time of plenty, and many Americans had begun to embrace Kennedy's dream of a better society founded on the best of the nation's ideals. After all, they reasoned, America could afford such a dream. The progress achieved on the materialistic side of the American Dream could be used to prop up the sagging idealistic side of the dream and attend to the needs and rights of all the people. "It was not long before a rights consciousness emerged that shook the surface calm of the American people."[17]

The assassination of John F. Kennedy was the first in a long series of disappointments that would slowly escort the baby boom generation from expectation to disappointment, from hope to despair, from faith to uncertainty, from idealism to cynicism. But this would take time, and in the meantime the new dream would live on. Only a year after Kennedy's tragic death, Lyndon Johnson announced the largest, most ambitious social program in the nation's history. "We have the opportunity," he told the American people in May of 1964, "to move not only toward the rich society and the powerful society, but upward to the Great Society. The Great Society rests on abundance and liberty for all. It demands an end to poverty and racial justice."[18] Here was a bold effort to reconcile the two faces of the American Dream; in true American fashion, the materialistic side of the dream would finance the idealistic side. Johnson's Great Society and his War on Poverty occasioned a period of governmental growth rivaled only by the New Deal era.[19] "Government liberates the individual from the enslaving forces of the environment," Johnson declared.[20] It was the beginning of an age of entitlements and state regulation. As the 1970s began Americans were turning to government for reasons that would have been formerly unthinkable.

It was also the beginning of an era of rising cynicism.[21] Racial tensions erupted, cities burned, and crime skyrocketed. The government seemed powerless to deal with these problems. Along the way, a youthful counterculture emerged that rejected almost everything the older generation held dear: money, success, education, marriage, law, religion, and so on. In and of itself this was not really so surprising. After all, this was the most coddled, most willfully confident, most self-possessed, most naïvely idealistic generation America had ever produced. But with the escalation of the Vietnam War, the gap between the espoused national objectives and the actual events in Asia soon became too large to overlook. Overwhelming disillusionment followed, and young people took to the streets in protest.

Still, the government continued to grow under Nixon. But the twin effects of Vietnam and Watergate shattered the faith that Americans had placed in government. Jobs became scarce, wages flattened, prices soared, interest rates rose, homes became hard to buy, cities decayed, the divorce rate skyrocketed, drug use increased, and crime escalated. New Deal, Fair Deal, New Frontier, Great Society, whatever the name, millions suddenly found the welfare state "dangerous to liberty, inimical to individualism and destructive of economic expansion."[22] Finally to the cheers of these new doubters, Ronald Reagan would assert, "Government is not the solution to our problems. Government is the problem." Under Reagan and Bush, attempts were made to tear down the regulatory infrastructure that had been erected during a century of liberal construction. This proved difficult. Nonetheless, if government was indeed the problem, the conservatives reasoned, then a return to the market place and *laissez faire* was in order. But, as the American experience had already illustrated in the Gilded Age and again in the 1920s, *laissez faire* could not succeed unless accompanied by an idealistic individualism that dreamed dreams of the common good. Acting alone, the materialistic side of the American Dream supported only by the unfettered individualism of material self-interest was not the key.

The American Dream was crumbling. Having traded their idealistic individualism for so many trinkets, Americans were powerless to affect change. Now, unable to buy back its bartered ideals with government programs, the vast, new, expectant generation that had seen itself as heir to the new American Dream of abundance was becoming cynical as none before it had been. The nation had come a long way indeed since Ralph Waldo Emerson wrote, "Society everywhere is in conspiracy against the manhood of each one of its members. Society is a joint-stock company, in which the members agree, for the better securing of bread to each shareholder, to surrender the liberty and culture of the eater."[23]

Part III:
The American Dream and Cynicism in America Today

The sea of faith
Was once, too, at the full and round earth's shore
Lay like the folds of a bright griddle furl'd.
But now I only hear
Its melancholy, long, withdrawing roar,
Retreating, to the breath
Of the night wind, down the vast edges drear
And the naked shingles of the world

Mathew Arnold
Dover Beach

8

The Causes of Cynicism in America

It is the theme of this book that cynicism in America today is the result of a shift in the American Dream. All men are in need of dreams to guide, motivate, and inspire them in their quests for better and more fulfilling lives. The nobler the dream, the potentially nobler and richer is the life of the dreamer. Nations, too, require dreams to define national objectives, to unite citizens around common goals, to define and solidify ideologies, and to inspire unified collective action. Like men, nations are measured by the nobility and viability of their dreams.

Predispositions

As the preceding chapters have illustrated, the entire epic of American history is a story of expanding expectations, a saga of a dream that grew greedy. Although ambitious, the first versions of the American Dream today appear childishly simple and naïve. In the beginning, the New World was a great green wilderness of dreams: dreams of new beginnings, of liberty, and of abundance. The early American Dream was the agrarian vision of a hardy new breed of self-reliant individuals who embraced hard work and sacrifice. It was built on the notion that with work, self-sufficiency, sobriety, thrift, initiative, moderation, and endurance the riches of a new land would be placed at the feet of the dreamer. This concept was more than a dream; it was an ethic, for it implied not only a possibility for material abundance, but also a path to a better, more moral life. Thus, the American Dream became a bifurcated dream;

one side aspired to material wealth while the other, supposedly complementary, side aspired to liberty, democracy, equality, the common good, and a new morality.

But as the new nation grew, it began to lose its simple rural character. Great cities sprang up and coarser strains of individualism began to inspire more acquisitive dreams, dreams that aspired to material wealth far beyond the modest hopes of America's first generations of republican yeoman farmers. In this atmosphere, the American ideals of liberty and democracy were often manipulated in support of material plunder. For many Americans, with the industrialization of America, the material side of the American Dream was realized, and with its fulfillment, the Dream itself began to change. The escalating expectations created by the success of American industry gave birth to the American Dream of progress.

This new dream included the notion that, with American know-how, initiative, and technological superiority, American material progress was inevitable—that each successive generation would be better off than the one before it. With continued success, the American Dream of progress slowly evolved in the minds of most Americans until it became the American Promise of progress. Amid soaring expectations, the enormous baby boom generation was born into an era of national industrial and economic dominance, world power, and patriotic self-righteousness. Here was the most expectant generation America had yet produced arriving on a stage that was set to disappoint. The whole of American history seemed to have occurred in order to predispose this generation to cynicism like none before it.

But there is more to America's predisposition to cynicism than history. The prosperity that came with industrialization had come at a numbing price. The Industrial Revolution had robbed the Western World of part of its very soul. Nowhere was this theft more poignant than in America, for here there had been no shared ethnicity, no common religion, no sense of historical heritage, no tradition of aristocracy, no social rigidity; here there had been only an idea, a vision, a dream.[1] The larcenies inflicted on America by urbanization, modernization, and industrialization have largely robbed the nation of her individualism and forever altered her most cherished dreams. For most, there remain only the hollow longings of modern consumerism and an unwholesome fetish for fad and celebrity. All but gone are individualism and the strict moral climate that surrounded the work ethic. Such notions "no longer fit the facts of . . . existence."[2] They have been rendered obsolete by the so-called "Modern Condition," which is characterized by dependency, hopelessness, alienation, and a new "Mass Society."

Like cynicism, the Modern Condition and the Mass Society have proved difficult concepts to pin down. Since 1966, Harris polls have attempted to measure alienation by having Americans evaluate statements like, "the people running the county don't really care what happens to me," "the rich get richer and the poor get poorer," "most people with power try to take advantage of people like myself." The average figure for those expressing disaffection on a combination of these items increased from 29 percent in 1966 to 60 percent in 1989.[3]

Other studies have attempted to assess the national mood, including Wrightsman's study of the "philosophies of human nature," which was designed to assess attitudes about trustworthiness and altruism (1964); Rosenberg's index of "faith in people," which attempts to measure attitudes about people's honesty, goodness, and generosity (1957); and Kanter and Mervis's surveys of attitudes and cynicism (1983). [4] All have painted a disturbing picture of America's reaction to the Modern Condition. Irving Howe describes Mass Society as a "half-welfare, half-garrison society" in which the population languishes. In place of initiative there is indifference, in place of action there is passivity, in place of opinion there is disinterest. Only a relic of the original American Dream remains, along with the ubiquitous American consumer, who is himself becoming "mass-produced like the products, diversions, and values he absorbs."[5] Traditional centers of authority like the family are losing their bind on individuals. Americans are adrift, powerless, without control; and public opinion today is largely artificially manufactured.[6] All the while, technology that had once promised so much suddenly seems distant, unfathomable, and arbitrary, while the dire prospects of the nuclear age lurk in the background. If not a part of cynicism itself, the Modern Condition has predisposed America to cynicism. As Peter Sloterdijk puts it, "The more modern society appears to be without [moral] alternatives, the more it will allow itself to be cynical."[7]

Faith Abused and Dreams Disappointed

With this understanding of America's cynical predispositions including our long national history of rising expectations, the unprecedented hopes of the recent generations, and the uncertainties and ambiguities of the Modern Condition, there remains only to inventory the American Dream in order to recount the corruptions and disappointments that lie at the root of cynicism in America. The more devout the faith, the more hopeful the expectation, and the more certain the promise, the more cynical are the betrayed.

The American Dream of Liberty. Despite so many apparent defeats and betrayals, the American Dream of liberty has remained surprisingly resilient. It just may yet be alive. Even in a cynical age, it may be out there lurking somewhere just beneath the surface. Still, today it is clear that it has lost some of its luster. There is little doubt that in revolutionary times Americans had a clear idea of what liberty meant. It was no vague term then. It meant "freedom under laws of [one's] . . . own making, and . . . the right to do anything that did not harm another." Today our definitions of liberty have "become fuzzy in the light of economic choice and social welfare."[8]

Nonetheless, liberty is one of those sacred catchwords that cynical politicians so often ingeniously employ to manipulate the masses. "Liberty wounded" is a "red shirt" waved by many a would-be American demagogue. Thus, the average American is cynically wary when he hears these words. In addition to these petty cynical dramas enacted around the word "liberty" today, our national disappointment in the American Dream of liberty and the corresponding cynicism concerning liberty in America stem from "the apprehension that the rational traditional balance between personal liberty and communal equality is being lost to gross polarization into rich and poor."[9]

The American Dream of Democracy. One need only consult recent polling records to find convincing evidence of the widespread loss of faith in democracy that characterizes the contemporary American mind. Today the United States has the lowest rate of voter participation of all the industrialized nations.[10] This erosion of faith is not a new trend. Many of the founding fathers were skeptical if not downright cynical, about the prospects for a democratic America. At the root of their fears was what they called "the tyranny of the majority." A century later, it was not the majority that threatened the American Dream, but rather the rising capitalist elite who were abusing our democratic institutions to such a degree that many Americans lost faith in the Dream of democracy.

Today a dull sense of political powerlessness infects the nation and breeds disappointment. For almost everyone, the hopeless complexity of American political machinery and the American political process are as baffling and as frustrating as they are sometimes comedic. Finally, for those who retain a glimmer of hope that their voice and their vote may actually count for something and that the mountains of bureaucracy can be scaled, there is increasing despair. Even when we were finally faced with a truly close election, a case where every single vote promised to carry great weight, there was the ignoble slapstick drama of the "hanging chad." It was enough to make anyone cynical. But beyond all of this, even if the checkered history of the American democratic circus fails to spark disillusionment and cynicism, the current state of affairs regarding political advertising and campaign funding will.

The American Dream of Equality. The "self-evident" truth that "all men are created equal" has been at the core of the American Dream of equality from the beginning. And from the very beginning it has been a dream disappointed. That such words could be employed by a nation that condoned slavery for nearly 100 years is itself the height of cynicism. Vernon Parrington reminds us that at the close of the American Revolution the dream of liberty was ascendant, but "humanitarian concepts of equality and fraternity found little response. . . ."[11] Likewise the fact that women were not considered even politically equal in America until 1920 ignites cynicism arising from a similar disappointment in the Dream of equality. Later in the century "separate but equal" was as cynical a turn of phrase as had ever been uttered. And despite all of the rhetoric and legislation of the last third of the twentieth century, America is still in significant part a racist country.

Cynicism defines racism. In the racist's heart is fear, a fearful mistrust of the motives of groups and individuals based on ethnic differences. What could be more cynical, except perhaps the fact that in order to justify their racism many Americans wave the flag of liberty, thus contaminating and disappointing the American Dream of liberty as well as the American Dream of equality. From the very beginning the

American Dream of equality has been the most disappointing dream of all.

The American Dream of Progress. The American

Dream of progress is our national impossible dream. At its heart is a utopian vision of perpetually increasing prosperity that promises that each succeeding generation will be materially better off than its predecessor. During the quarter century that followed World War II, America experienced uninterrupted economic growth, accelerated educational development, breakthrough technological advancement, and expanded international influence.

Built on both a stubborn faith in the "American system" and an unrealistic belief in the growing myths of American know-how, technological superiority, and business acumen, the American Dream of progress seduced the enormous baby boom generation, thus fostering soaring national expectations that far surpassed the dreams of any previous generation. Such wild dreams were bound to disappoint. Their ideals shattered by assassinations, political lies, and an unjust war, the baby boomers went on to face a stagnating economy, skyrocketing interest rates, and a sputtering job market. In the wake of such a disappointing end to the unbridled expectations of an entire generation, the baby boomers became the mothers and fathers of modern cynicism in America.

At the root of the American Dream of progress was a new Doctrine of Change. This doctrine insisted that all the changes that rode on the cresting wave of American technology and science were changes that worked for the good because they increased material prosperity. Few looked up to notice America's aging political institutions, social structures, and value systems as they tottered under the weight of such rapid change. In the end, technological change created not only material progress, but also "future shock."[12] The numbing pace of change itself would become a destroyer of many American Dreams and thus itself a cause of cynicism.

The American Dream of Moral Fitness. With its Puritan beginnings and its deep-rooted work ethic, the American Dream of moral fitness lies at the very core of the American mind. It is not just a product of a healthy respect for the rule of law; it is an ingrained national ethic that goes all the way back to the first frontier. A fair day's work for a fair day's pay, the sanctity of a man's word, unswerving loyalty, manners, personal sacrifice, an unshakable belief in the fact that "a deal" is a indeed "a deal," "look-a-man-in-the-eye," a firm hand shake, old debts repaid: all were part of a simple, straightforward, "Gary Cooper" image of fair play—a national preoccupation with "doing the right thing." But, sadly, the American Dream of moral fitness is today becoming the American Myth of moral fitness.

We hear a great deal about "family values" today, but the complexity of modern society has created ambiguities and even rendered many of the old values obsolete. To be sure, this is difficult to measure, but the lack of simple civility in public places and the seemingly total absence of personal courtesy, even in children in the street, today invite the cynic's eye. In *Dialogic Civility in a Cynical Age* Ronald Arnett and Pat Arneson mourn the passing of the American Dream of moral fitness, "Many lives seem to lack 'everyday virtues' of honesty, loyalty, manners, work and restraint. From this lack of moral victory . . . has emerged not compromise, but instead a routine cynical appraisal of our modern social condition."[13] Everybody knows that cynicism thrives in a moral vacuum.

The American Dream of the Land. In the very beginning the first American Dream had been the land itself— a mythical vision come to life, a tangible promise of a new beginning. For centuries the American frontier was both a dream and a shaper of dreams. But 400 years after its discovery, the frontier was at an end, and the nation was being transformed. A nation of farms was reshaped into a nation of factories. What was once rural was suddenly urban. After her long agrarian upbringing, America found herself cut off from the land; the machine was loose in the garden.

This national separation from the land eroded the sturdy individualism upon which so many American dreams had been built. The American Dream of the land had once been a dream come true. By the middle of the twentieth century, it had once again become only a myth. The roots of American cynicism are planted deep in this nostalgic soil.

The American Dream of Work.

The industrialization and urbanization of the nation not only disappointed the American Dream of the land, it also disappointed the American Dream of work. The ideal that there is an intrinsic moral value in work is part of our Puritan heritage, and along with Puritan self-denial, thrift, moderation, and patience, it was quickly incorporated into a robust American frontier ethic that also espoused industry, self-discipline, initiative, and endurance. This new American Work Ethic saw these as moral qualities and clearly stated that with their application, anyone could prosper in the new land. But with industrialization came the division of labor, and work was transformed. No longer an uplifting, individual, personal expression, it became numbing, conforming, interdependent drudgery. Gone were earlier notions of work as craft and calling. For generations of Americans, the American Dream of work had meant the idea of delayed gratification, loyalty, and sacrifice for the future. But with the coming of the machine, these ideas began to unravel.

In his study *Blue Monday* Robert Eisenberger cites a number of modern factors that work to weaken the traditional

American work ethic, including the depersonalization of big corporations, further fractionalization in the division of labor, the emphasis on speed and efficiency over quality, the cultural allure of leisure and sensual satisfaction as opposed to work as a means toward individual fulfillment, and our present-day worship of wealth. In conclusion Eisenberger adds, "Acceptance of a present-oriented life style involving sensual gratifications undermines the tolerance for hard work needed to achieve long-term goals." Today most workers are transient, and for many Americans work is no longer viewed as a means of self-fulfillment. Millions are cynical about work, believing that "those who worked hard and played by the rules wound up with the short end of the stick. And those who flouted the rules got away with it." Cynicism also abounds as workers cease to trust the motives of managers and the wisdom and benevolence of capitalistic corporate culture.[14]

The American Economic Dream. From the beginning, the American Economic Dream was built upon the broad shoulders of the Myth of Capitalism. Led first by Jefferson, the idealistic forces of liberty sided with Adam Smith, espousing an unfettered *laissez faire* approach. Adam Smith put forward the idea that the common economic good was eventually best served when workers and entrepreneurs alike were left totally free to pursue their own perceived self-interests. Hamilton, the Federalists and their followers favored checks and controls. Indeed, there turned out to be more things in heaven and earth than were dreamt of in Adam Smith's philosophies. At its root of *laissez faire* was brutal economic Darwinism, a kind of economic anarchy. Smith failed to fully account for the coming power of the machine and the societal upheaval created by urbanization and the factory.

The American Economic Dream was soon disappointed by the unmasking of the ruthless, grasping nature of unfettered capitalism. In the period after the Civil War, unchecked American capitalism led to an unprecedented period of exploitation, manipulation, and corruption. Cynicism followed disappointment and continued as government sought to rein in the raging capitalistic beast. Government controls brought more disappointment and new cynicisms.

Today America's faith in the economy is at an all time low. Inflation, stagflation, deflation, trade deficits, soaring national debt, insider trading, the S & L debacle, stock market volatility, rising gas and health care costs, all add to the uncertainty. As Jeffery Goldfarb puts it, "With stock market speculation, junk bonds and corporate takeovers, capitalism has reached its logical conclusion. Now it is not simply that the workers are alienated from the fruits of their labors, capital accumulation has become distinct from production and entrepreneurship."[15] Confidence in business leadership sank from 70 percent in the 1960s to 7 percent in 1989.[16]

According to demographers and pollsters Donald Kanner and Philip Mirvis's 1989 investigations, "business gets lower marks than government in ratings of public approbation."[17] People feel ripped off. It is clear to almost everyone that quality is missing from many American products. The very concept of "planned obsolescence" evokes cynicism. Most Americans will even begrudgingly admit that the Japanese (once the joke of the consumer manufacturing world) now consistently make better products than we do. The American Dream of material wealth may still be alive and well, but the economic Dream that supports it is seriously ailing, and many today are cynical about the economy. They nod, smirk, and wink knowingly as the salaries of top executives continue to rise beyond their already immoral levels.

The American Dream of Government. As the
preceding brief history clearly confirms, the United States fed-

eral government has been experiencing near exponential growth since the beginning of the twentieth century. This growth is the result of three modern ideological forces. First, the ideals of a modern welfare state insist that government has a duty to see to the well being of the less fortunate members of society. Second, increased emphasis on the doctrine of rights makes government responsible for the creation and enforcement of laws designed to ensure the rights of citizens and groups of citizens. And third, there is a general modern trend away from local prerogatives and toward centralized federal control of governmental functions. Despite the nobility of such ideals, the tendency of government has been to reach out and engross power, even if it has to trample upon the rights of individuals to do so. When it does, the stage is set for another kind of cynicism. We have created an increasingly large, fumbling, inefficient institution in order to see to the well being of the poor and to the rights of the dispossessed. But this ungainly institution is, by its very nature, compelled to secure and enhance its own power, even at the expense of those it was chartered to protect.

The tendency of bureaucracy is well known: each government agency remains loyal to its own self-interest and its own aspirations to growth and power. Each department "keeps to itself," "feathers its own nest," "plays it close to the vest," all the while distrusting other departments. Each agency seeks the power that comes with growth, when, in the name of the public interest, it should be seeking efficiency. Is it any wonder Americans are cynical?

Daniel Yankelovich, a noted social analyst, reported in 1978 "We have seen a steady rise of mistrust in our national institutions. Trust in government declined dramatically from almost 80% in the late 50s to about 33% in 1976."[18] In *The Cynical Americans* Kanter and Mirris point to "Harris polls that show that confidence in the Supreme Court, Congress, and the executive branch, in state and local government . . . declined precipitously from 1966 to 1974 to 1986."[19] Still government continues to grow. The statistics are even more depressing today.[20] We have come a long, long way from Thomas Paine's guiding observation, "That government is best which governs least."

The American Dream of World Leadership and Power.

After World War II there was a growing feeling in America that, not only was America the most powerful nation in the world, it was also the best nation in the world. This blindly nationalistic notion had been incubating since the beginning of the century, and with victories on both side of the globe in the 1940s, Americans came to believe that the American Dream of progress would eventually and inevitably extend to all the nations of the world. To some extent this dream was well meaning despite its conceit. But to the extent that American policy abroad worked to extend American influence at the expense of the self-determination of other nations, it became one of America's most cynical notions. It preached freedom, but only *our* kind of freedom.

This was essentially a self-negating, fundamentalist notion. It was particularly dangerous in the third world, where institutions strong enough to support democracy and free markets were not always in place. Certainly the old image of the "ugly American" had its roots in this kind of arrogance, which was also characterized by a general lack of respect for the culture, institutions, and traditions of other nations. Nationalistic notions of American superiority led to inflexibilities in foreign policy, and resulted in debacles in Vietnam, Latin America, and likely in the Middle East as well. The enormous disappointment and cynicism that followed in the wake of the disasters wrought by the American Dream of world power is difficult to measure.

The American Dream of Science and Technology.

Closely related to the American Dream of world leadership and power is the American Dream of science and technology. From the beginnings of the Industrial Revolution, American contributions to science and technology have been impressive. Eli Whitney's ideas regarding interchangeable parts are the linchpin of the modern factory system; Thomas Edison's achievements are unmatched anywhere; America's pioneering efforts in aviation and in the development of the automobile are significant, although overblown in the national mind. And of course there is the groundbreaking research that led to the development of nuclear energy, which most Americans will hastily claim as our own despite the fact that most of the pioneering theoretical work was spearheaded by European émigrés. On top of all this there is the historical fact that American industry miraculously blossomed from obscurity into world dominance in only a handful of decades.

With so much to brag about, Americans were quick to move well beyond simple pride of accomplishment and fabricate another fantastic national dream of superiority. Building on the old notion of "Yankee ingenuity," as well as the myths of American "know-how" and the national "can do" mindset, the American Dream of science and technology asserted that not only was America the historical world leader in these areas, but that it was our national destiny to continue this leadership. The widespread notion of continuing American technological supremacy was based on a general "gut feeling" that somehow Americans were just "better at this kind of stuff" and that the free, democratic, capitalistic atmosphere in the United States provided a better nursery for new technological ideas and applications.

This did not turn out to be the case, as Sputnik was to so traumatically illustrate. Some Americans still refused to acknowledge Japanese and European equity, if not superiority in many areas. The rest were surprised and disappointed when the Japanese auto industry swept to world dominance based on better-engineered, more robust products, or when European aviation contractors began to compete head-to-head with Boeing and McDonald Douglas. The American Dream of scientific and technological superiority is just another nationalistic arrogance that is destined to disappoint; just another breeding ground for cynicism.

With its insistence on inevitable dominance, the American Dream of science and technology is also very closely related to the American Dream of progress. In fact, the American Dream of progress is, at least in part, built upon our national faith in technological superiority. The Dream holds that that each generation will continue to be better off than preceding generations because continued advances in technology will lead to increased efficiency. In turn, increased efficiency will lead to increased prosperity and leisure, and perpetuate a progressively healthier and increasingly happier population. Even if this fantasy were possible, what the Dream fails to consider is the cost of this technology-driven prosperity in terms of the on-going surrender to the "Modern Condition;" the loss of individualism, the decline of the family, the erosion of traditional values, the numbing monotony of urban existence, the growing pressures of modern life, and the national tendency toward cynicism.

The American Dream of Education.

The American Dream of education has existed since the earliest days of the American colonies. It is tied to the Enlightenment idea of the perfectibility of man, and it insists, "investment in people is the most essential way for a society to devote its resources. . . ."[21] As the modern age unfolded, Americans came to rightly believe that "increases in productivity . . . come directly from the size of the national investment in education . . ."[22] According to John Kenneth Galbraith, "a dollar . . . invested in the intellectual development of human beings will regularly bring greater increase in a nation's income than a dollar devoted to railways, dams, machine tools, or other tangible capital goods."[23]

Based on this reality, the Dream of education came to become part of the fallacious American Dream of progress, asserting that higher education will inevitably avail more and more Americans to a piece of the American pie of plenty. The new Dream of education goes so far as to assure the young that education itself is the key to success. As noble as this may sound, it has not proved to be the case in recent years. Modern generations of Americans are so immersed in the Dream of education, that once out of college, they expect American big business to beat a path to their doorstep. When this fails to happen and menial work is the only alternative, disappointment sets in along with drudgery. Cynicism follows.

There is yet another side to the American Dream of education, having to do with the content of American institutional learning. From the earliest levels, children are taught the American Dream of progress along with a ludicrously revisionist version of American history, society, and politics. Although couched in the language of idealism, this line of teaching is often nothing less than a blatant form of nationalist propaganda, aimed at indoctrinating young people with regard to the rightness of American ideals, the superiority of American business and technology, and the material value of education itself. When these teachings later fail to fit reality, cynicism follows.

The American Dream of Family. The Dream of family has deep roots in the American tradition. From the very beginning, the family was the irreducible core institution of a nation of farmers. In the early days, the family was not only the primary American social unit; it was the primary economic unit as well. With the coming of industrialization and urbanization, the family became a sort of fortress, an oasis in a harsh environment, not only providing nurture, but also safety, trust, loyalty, and security. Today the American family is struggling. Many still cling to traditional family structures, loyalties, and values, but the modern ravages of abandonment, divorce, broken homes, single parents, teenage pregnancy, family abuse, and latch-key children constantly chip away at this once nearly unassailable institution. Even for traditional American families, the time-honored patterns of life have changed.

The modern urban world allows little room for old-style family life. As a result many Americans are today adrift without the once-dependable lifeboat of family ties. The void left by the disappearance of the traditional American family is today the birthplace of modern feelings of isolation and hopelessness. In it there lurks a growing contemporary moral vacuum, an atmosphere in which cynicism thrives. The demise of the American family is particularly disillusioning for the baby boomers, indoctrinated as they all were by *Leave It to Beaver*.

The American Dream of Freedom of Religion.

Beyond the American Dream of the land, the American Dream of freedom of religion was perhaps the first American Dream. Unlike so many of the other American Dreams, the Dream of freedom of religion is today alive and well. For a brief period, it appeared that God might indeed be dead in America, but He has been resurrected. Given the uncertainty of the times, this is not surprising. In fact, in many cases the same ingredients that combine to create cynicism can also combine to create fundamentalism. America stands at a crossroads. After so many disappointments, so many American dreams corrupted, and in the face of the hopelessness, alienation, and uncertainty of the Modern Condition, some turn to cynicism, too little faith, while others embrace fundamentalism, too much faith. They are damned either way.

The Standardized American Dream. Despite the crumbling fate of the idealistic side of the American Dream, certain parts of its materialistic side are still in place. Despite difficult and uncertain times, despite grave suspicions regarding the integrity of the American Dream of progress, the media-driven Standardized American Dream is still alive and well. A good job, a family, two cars, and a house in the suburbs may be a more elusive dream than it was a few decades ago, but it is nonetheless still a reachable goal, an attainable dream. In fact, this "standardized" list still describes the goal of most Americans today. But today Americans have to work twice as hard to maintain the Standardized American Dream. And all the while the Modern Condition is closing in. Family life is a shamble of discord and miscommunication; the house and cars are mortgaged to the hilt, and most have no idea exactly how they will sustain their dreams in the near future, to say nothing of how they will survive in their old age. The Standardized American Dream is a Faustian bargain: a house in the suburbs in exchange for one's individual identity and hopes for self-fulfillment. The modern name for the ancient cynical Mephistopheles who brokers this modern day bargain is "television."

Cynicism and the American Media

The American media creates and stimulates widespread cynicism in four ways.

In *Television Myth and the American Mind,* Hal Himmelstein insists that many of the myths that sustain our society today are "embedded into our collective subconscious" by television. Foremost among these media-reinforced myths is the "myth of eternal progress," characterized by "the economic expansion of society and the growth of personal material compensations." According to Himmelstein, the media's fundamental aim is to lead the nation to "unbridled consumption" and an "advanced state of acquisitiveness." Television accomplishes this not only through advertising, but also through carefully selected and specifically focused programming. According to Himmelstein, such media manipulations are both "stultifying and controlling," bound as they are, not to the spectator, but to the consumer; not to art, but to the product; not to enlightenment, but to profitability. Sadly, as we have noted, the American Dream of perpetual progress is a transparent Ponzi scheme that is bound to disappoint, and thus, the perpetuation of this myth by the American media serves only to increase our inevitable disappointment and to deepen our resulting cynicism.[24]

The second way in which the American media creates and stimulates cynicism has to do with the content and packaging of information and entertainment. Peter Sloterdijk observes that a considerable part of our media "serves nothing other than the hunger for misadventure."[25] News is measured by its entertainment value, which is generally derived from the exploitation of catastrophe; the entertainment value of drama is often derived from violence, sensationalism, scandal, and the trickery of special effects. After repeated exposure to this over-the-top kind of entertainment, viewers become jaded. They soon know all of TV's seedy tricks by heart, and an increasingly cynical America eventually comes to view sensationalism, catastrophe, scandal, and trickery as just so much background noise. In *Looking Back*, Joyce Maynard relates the story of taking her four-year-old daughter, Hanna, to the circus:

> We are cynics who see the trap door in the magic
> show, the pillow stuffing in the Salvation Army Santa

Clauses, the camera tricks in TV commercials. . . .
We watched what must have been two dozen clowns
pile out of a Volkswagen without Hanna's knowing
what the point of it all was. It isn't just the knowledge that they emerge from a trap door in the saw-
dust that keeps Hanna from looking up, either. Even
if she didn't know the trick, she wouldn't care.[26]

In *For Common Things,* Jedediah Purdy points to a third
way in which the nation's relentless media has rendered many
Americans jaded. He explains, "We have been prepared by
years of exposure to idealized portrayals of the moments that
make each person's life unique. . . ." The combined effect of
these seemingly endless media portrayals has been to "render
cliché nearly everything anyone would feel it important to say."
As we become more sophisticated viewers of these portrayals, "we begin to doubt the significance of our own private
words and lives." Purdy's ironist, whom we have already un-
masked for the cynic that he is, thus perceives the world as
"grown old, flat and sterile." Nothing ever surprises him. Everything he encounters is "a remake, a re-release, a ripoff, or a
rerun." He has seen it all before. He perceives triteness in his
every word, therefore he subtly insists on the inadequacy of
each sentence as he speaks it.[27]

The fourth way in which the American media creates
and stimulates widespread cynicism has to do with the way
the media floods our consciousness. As Sloterdijk puts it, "For
the consciousness that informs itself in all directions, everything becomes problematic and inconsequential. . . ." Here is
the cynicism of the "matter-of-fact," a diffuse, omnipresent
cynicism that cuts deep into American life. Again Sloterdijk:
"Our minds are trained to scan and comprehend an encyclo-
pedically broad scale of irrelevancies – in which the irrelevance
of a single item comes not so much from itself but from be-

ing arranged in the flood of information from the media."[28] We are asked to untangle and evaluate a flickering web made up of the important and the unimportant as they are ceaselessly paraded before us. Ill equipped for such a daunting task, we eventually perceive only equivalence and thus slowly sink into cynical indifference.

The American media (especially television) not only creates and nurtures cynical forces in our society but is itself a cynical force in our society. Television is a wasteland of cynical themes, a "barrage of hype and hope orchestrated by advertising, programming, preaching, politicking and self-help enterprises never before experienced in such concentrated doses and with such graphic delivery systems." The media is a multi-ring circus starring the twin disasters of advertising and pop culture, hawking "possessions and celebrity routinely as if they were imperatives."[29] TV and movies project moral ambiguity in their portrayals of modern society as a dishonest, violent jungle. Pop lyrics defame time-honored institutions. Politicians mouth platitudes that neither they nor their listeners believe. The sporting scene no longer appears to focus on competition, but rather on an endless pageant of gangster millionaires addicted to drugs.

Against this backdrop how can we not turn to cynicism? After all, the cynic suffers no disillusionment. He discounts both the media and the message.

9

The Effects of Cynicism in America

Today cynicism is epidemic in America, and its effects are potentially ruinous. Like a crippling disease, cynicism spreads slowly, insidiously, and silently as it disables. The modern cynic is generally melancholy and withdrawn, although at times he can also be outgoing, charming, attractive, and even funny. But in the end, he withdraws to his unassailable towers of cynicism. His rhetoric is alluring, especially in uncertain times, when many seek cynicism's unique protection from the pain of disillusionment. Cynicism is especially disabling in a democracy where coalition, community, consensus, and good faith are critical to the operation of its political, social, and economic institutions. The cynic scoffs at such concepts and mocks their idealistic underpinnings as well as any efforts to more forward, or for than matter, backward.

The Sword and the Shield

As we have noted cynicism can be either "wielded like a sword or held up like a shield." As Kanter and Mirvis put it, it is both "a reaction to and a barrier against culturally induced and socially reinforced hopes that have been dashed." The cynic can be aggressive or passive; assertively offensive or reflexively defensive; outwardly hostile, forceful, sarcastic, or blunt; or inwardly withdrawn, melancholy, aloof, or detached. Many cynics exhibit both sides of the cynical split personality.[1]

Take for example, the case of H. L. Mencken. Arguably one the most influential Americans of his era, Mencken was both slashing kynic and withdrawn cynic. His criticism of

American life and institutions was fearless. For Mencken, nothing was sacred save the truth. He slashed away at democracy, Christianity, and virtually all of America's most revered ideals. But after each brilliant thrust, he could only turn away and laugh. As Louis Kronenberger observes:

> The upshot of [Mencken's] unsparing diagnosis—
> —which in theory constituted a kind of wholesale
> muckraking——was not a general movement to-
> ward reform, but a special movement toward with-
> drawal. It fostered the cult of the civilized minor-
> ity. In the thick of the blistering charges against
> American life in general, Mencken somehow con-
> trived to make the individual reader feel exempt for
> the indictment, an *âme bien née* who belonged on
> the side of Mencken and the angels. Thus, the situ-
> ation from the onset was ironical. Mencken, expos-
> ing the ghastly inadequacies of all matters of pub-
> lic interest, encouraged his readers to be too snob-
> bish to give a damn about them. He insisted he
> could offer no remedy and was amused that he
> should be expected to. Those whom he influenced
> at once accepted his conclusions and turned their
> backs on the national plight. . . .

Kronenberger concludes, "[Mencken's] tone at length became one of unredeemed cynicism."[2]

Most cynics today have forsaken the sword in favor of the shield. Kynical performance is rare today. There is no energy left for parades or protests or sarcasm. Today most cynics seek anonymity. They set themselves apart from the world of action and look down on events in a detached way. They are smug cowards, unwilling to risk so much as getting their hands dirty. Unlike the detached ironist, the cynic exists in the knowledge that it is pointless to have faith in anything but the self. The modern cynic is a mass character in a mass society, "moving toward a quiet desert . . . where men will forget their passions and moral and spiritual restlessness. . . ."[3] The effect of this migration will be political, social, and economic catatonia. Cynicism is numbing, disabling, paralyzing, an anesthetizer for progress.

Cynicism and the Status Quo

As we have noted, "Mocking cynicism" works to halt efforts toward meaningful change by suggesting that any such efforts are idealistic or even naïve.[4] For the mocking cynic the knowledge that life is a sham appears "so universal that alternatives no longer exist."[5] "Matter-of-fact" cynics are often so blind as to fail to recognize the difference between irrelevancies and matters of import urgently demanding attention and response. In these and many other ways, modern cynicism imparts a quality of motionlessness to everything it touches. Cynicism in America today works to preserve the status quo. The process is often a circular one like the political loop William Chaloupka describes in *Everybody Knows*. According to Chaloupka, cynical Americans generally avoid politics because it seems to "move forward through sleight of hand, indirection, paradox and intended confusion of sign and substance."[6] Cynics in power use this misdirection and confusion to manipulate citizens into "letting the rulers rule," thus increasing cynicism among the masses, and providing further opportunities for manipulation. This circular nature makes some things both causes and effects of cynicism.

Another example of this kind of circularity is described by Daniel Boorstin in his critique of the American news media. According to Boorstin, the media is so attuned to the cynicism of its audience that it must present not so much something that "accurately describes the situation but something that sounds true." It is a cynical world indeed when the public is so distrustful of what it hears and reads that it must evaluate everything according to its credibility. As Boorstin puts it, ". . . we live in a world of pseudo-events and quasi-information, in which the air is saturated with statements that are neither true nor false but merely credible."[7] Democracy thrives on the truth, and the media cynically gives us only half-truths, thus further weakening public trust and breeding more cynicism. Here again cynicism stands in the path of progress.

Cynicism and the American Dream

Cynicism subverts, resists, undermines, and sabotages the American Dream. All dreams require belief, and cynicism denies belief. Today, Chaloupka notes, "Belief has become less possible, exhausted by conflict, by the enormity of the demands placed on the system [and on the Dream] . . . and by increasing opportunities for successful political and journalistic use of cynicism. . . . [Belief] has ceased to be the only practical master strategy for life in a democratic society."[8] But cynicism is not really an alternative strategy to belief or to anything else for that matter; it is a road that leads to no alternatives, a perpetual dead-end.

Cynicism and the American Dream are locked in a downward spiral. A large portion of the old American Dream is no longer relevant in today's world. This creates frustration and disappointment and finally begets cynicism, which destroys belief. Without belief the American Dream descends into further irrelevance, thus creating more disappointment and more cynics. What is needed to break the cycle of cynicism in America is not more belief to breed more disappointment and more cynics. What is needed is a new American Dream.

Part IV:
A New American Dream

We must imagine some end to life that
transcends our own allotment of days and
hours if we are to keep at bay the dim,
back-of-the-mind suspicion that one may
be adrift in the world.

Clifford Greetz

Religion as a Cultural System

10

A Cure for Cynicism in America

It is difficult to write about cynicism in America without appearing overly negative about America. To be sure, today there is grave trouble in the so-called "Land of the Free." Today cynicism threatens to disable the political, social, and economic machinery that made this country what it is. Yet, we still have many strengths. As Winston Churchill reportedly once said to a critic, "Any fool can see what's *wrong* with it. Can't you see what's *right* with it?" Indeed, there is still a great deal that is "right with America." There is still hope. There is still opportunity. There is still the freedom to rise. But if we are to save all this from the ravages of cynicism, we have work to do.

As with any job, the best way to begin is with a clear, concise assessment of the task at hand, including the identification of any problem areas that may surface during such an assessment. We must then confront these problem areas head on. If the foregoing history and analysis of cynicism and the American Dream leads us to any conclusions in this regard, it is that the American Dream has acted as a powerful force in the shaping of all aspects of American political, social, and economic life, and that in recent years many aspects of the old American Dream no longer seem to dovetail with the evolving realities of modern life in America. This is to say that our dreams and expectations have remained relatively unchanged, while the world in which we live has changed radically. Today old institutions and old values no longer function smoothly, and many of the old dreams are no longer within our grasp. As we have seen, the result has been feelings of disappointment, helplessness, powerlessness, and, finally, cynicism.

Our history also illustrates that over the years, many new codicils and amendments were added to the old American Dream, and in the last half of the twentieth century, many of these began to take on the appearance of promises, rights, and entitlements—not dreams at all, but things that would eventually be taken for granted. Among these was the inevitability of American progress, superiority, and affluence.

Thus, as the post-modern era unfolded, we painted ourselves into a corner. Our dreams, soaring expectations, and sense of superiority no longer agreed with reality. The resulting disappointment is "not a product of failure, but of the absence of success commensurate with the goals in mind." The American Dream has "not adequately allowed for limited success," or perhaps our dreams have not defined success correctly and realistically. Whatever the case, "the discrepancy between the utopia promised and the reality delivered" has become too great. When this happens, Zachary Karabell reminds us, "the paradigm will collapse under the weight of its own expectations."[1]

In *The American Dream: A Short History of an Idea that Shaped a Nation,* Jim Cullen offers a sobering summary. The American Dream began with a "people who denied that their efforts could control their fates, moves through their successors who later declared independence to get that chance, to heirs who elaborated a gospel of self-help, promising they could shape their fate with effort, and ends with a people who long to achieve dreams without having to make any effort at all." If this is a true reading of our history, and if, as Arnett and Arneson assert, "cynicism springs from overt deception and rhetoric that exceeds what can realistically be accomplished," then no wonder we are cynical.[2]

So the clear, concise assessment of the task at hand is

this: we must openly address cynicism in America; we must come to grips with the Modern Condition; and we must restore faith in a workable American Dream.

For Common Things

Social criticism today rarely confronts cynicism realistically. The intransigence of the American cynic is generally ignored or grossly underestimated. Likewise, few actually confront the Modern Condition as a permanent fact of life. In the rare cases that cynicism and the Modern Condition are acknowledged, the response is generally an attempt to alter the present state of affairs by attempting some kind of "faith healing" or by applying other equally out-of-date remedies. These "cures" often involve idealistic calls for community and renewed commitment. Many critics cling to the solutions of an America that is no more, solutions based on a vanishing individualism, archaic agrarian values, and a disappearing Puritan work ethic. Perhaps most importantly, no one dares assail the traditional American Dream, which is widely viewed as sacrosanct, an integral, unalterable part of the national soul.

Accordingly, most constructive contemporary social criticism fails to move the American cynic. In a cynical nation, simple calls for responsibility, values, and belief, no matter how wise, logically argued, or articulately phrased, fall upon deaf ears. The modern American social critic must first address cynicism and all of its underlying causes, before his eloquent calls for community, commitment, responsibility, and hope can even pretend to resound with anything other than a dull thud.

Take the case of young Jedediah Purdy. His recent book, *For Common Things,* is an impassioned plea for "attention to things that we have been neglecting," and for "the active preservation of things that we must hold in common." Taking a page from Emerson (or perhaps from Richard Rorty) Purdy tells us, "The party of hope cannot continue unless it is also the party of memory." Purdy is sure that there are things in our pasts that we all share, memories "that reassure us of, or keep us from entirely surrendering, the possibility of trust, or confidence in reality." In short, Purdy believes we all share memories that can save us from cynicism, but we have just been neglecting them.[3]

Mr. Purdy comes by this idea honestly. His background is quite extraordinary, and he insists on flaunting the "credential" of his rural West Virginia childhood. In truth, Purdy's childhood was a great deal more than just rural. It was reactionary. Seeking to "pick a small corner of the world and make it as sane as possible,"[4] his parents simply "dropped out" as the phrase went in the early 1970s. Home-schooled and raised on a remote subsistence farm in the Appalachians, Purdy describes his father plowing with draft horses. The fact is that young Jedediah Purdy grew up in a facsimile of the America of the nineteenth century, isolated, agrarian, and keenly self-reliant. Purdy's childhood is an anachronism, an artifact of the American frontier, even harkening all the way back to Thomas Jefferson's beloved "yeoman farmers," who were to be the perpetual guardians of democracy, individualism, and liberty.

Thus, it is no coincidence that the cures that Mr. Purdy puts forward in *For Common Things,* rely on frontier values: responsibility, work, community, and self-reliance. He tells us that he grew up "knowing exactly what could be relied upon," that his childhood experience was an "exercise in trust." Despite an upbringing so unique that he shares memories in common with perhaps only the Amish, Purdy insists that although his childhood experiences are "in some ways anomalous," they are also "typical." As unlikely as this many sound, he is convinced that, deep inside, we all share similar memories that affirm a "confidence in the reality," and that we all maintain, "private, half-secret repositories of hope and trust."[5]

To be sure, many Americans have innocent, fond, and even loving childhood memories. Most were nurtured in an atmosphere of relative security, warmth, and expectation. Nonetheless, the America that spawned the baby boom and subsequent generations is a long distance from the America of the frontier. Today the frontier is more than one hundred years gone. In its place cities sprawl, factories toil, televisions blare, and shopping malls cater to a population of devoted consumers. The values of the frontier no longer dovetail with modern reality. Simple self-reliance has turned into complex interdependence. Individualism has been engulfed in a mass society. For many, work holds little reward beyond a wage. The family is dissolving as the center of moral life. In place of community we find estrangement, alienation, and isolation. This is the so-called Modern Condition, characterized by moral ambiguity, a run-away industrial world where uncertainty is the only certainty. Against this backdrop, few childhoods these days, no matter how loving, are "an exercise in trust" or result in a "perfect confidence." Children are remarkably astute, and, no matter how sheltered, how initially hopeful, most Americans gleaned modern lessons at an early age, lessons of lingering nameless dread, of wary mistrust and of the cynicism so common in today's cold, unflinching world.

Modern Americans do not choose civic neglect, political inattention, public irresponsibility, and cynicism. They are conditioned to them by constant disappointment that flows from the failure of outdated values and dreams. Nonetheless, Purdy clings to the idea that somewhere deep inside everyone there remains a reluctant hope which if kindled by common concerns, can again burn as a renewed commitment to "Common Things." His conclusion assails us with high-minded platitudes. "Work should affirm our lives as things decent in possibility. . . ." "The alchemy of love and responsibility belongs at the heart of a renewed commitment to the commons." "The dignity that I have observed has to do with the harmony of commitment, knowledge and work," and so on.[6] Few of us would dispute these things, but the real question is this: if we have any latent hope at all, how are we to rekindle it in order to begin to act as Mr. Purdy would have us act? Of course, a real cynic would never bother to ask such a question.

For Common Things likewise fails to ask this question, thus it fails to suggest any answer. There is no plan for the revival of political institutions, no motion toward specific organizations or methods of reform. There is only a vague sense that we might some day experience some kind of personal conversion or a sudden re-awakening of hope. This is not likely in the case of the American cynic. Jedediah Purdy's concept of "skeptical irony" is insightful indeed, but, as we have already discovered, his ironist is really just a cynic in transparent disguise. *For Common Things* simply refuses to acknowledge the issue of cynicism. In the end, we are left with only an articulate but shallow call for belief, and as we shall now see, when it comes to cynicism, there is a big problem with calls for more belief.

The Problem with Belief

If the true nature of cynicism fits any of the "standard definitions" ("a condition of lost belief," "faith abused," "a disposition to disbelieve" and so on), then the cure for cynicism must be renewed belief. Indeed, "more belief" has been the traditional American panacea. As Chaloupka notes:

> Every diagnosis of cynicism renews a call to belief, and Americans at least talk believer talk. One moralist after another, whether political televangelist, professor, or communicator announces that we must reestablish belief and reconstruct community values that have fallen into disrepair. . . . If the problem is cynicism, the solution must be belief—in lead-

ership, education, obedience, and responsible application of moral criticism.[7]

The laundry list of authors and thinkers who continually offer belief as a remedy for cynicism seems as endless as
their suggested cures seem hollow. A few additional examples
will suffice.

Some take a noble, patriotic tone but, beyond the beauty
of their words and the patriot's emotional, evangelical faith in
his country, which endures against all odds, offer little practical substance. In *You Can't Go Home Again,* Thomas Wolfe writes:

> I believe that we are lost here in America, but I be-
> lieve that we shall be found. . . . I think the true
> discovery of America is before us. I think the true
> fulfillment of our spirit, of our people, of our mighty
> and immortal land, is yet to come. I think the true
> discovery of our democracy is still before us. And I
> think that all of these things are as certain as the
> morning, as inevitable as noon. I think I speak for
> most men living when I say that our America is Here,
> is Now, and beckons on before us, and that this glo-
> rious assurance is not only our living hope, but our
> dream to be accomplished.

Others are the work of the great observers of social
trends like Daniel Yankelovich, who, in *New Rules,* views the
American quest for self-fulfillment as a possible starting point
for a "search for a new American way of life," which in turn
may shape a new American social ethic to replace the old Puritan work ethic. The new ethic, which Yankelovich calls the
"ethic of commitment," will exist in a "new realism" that will
include "renewed emphasis on sharing, giving, committing,
sacrificing, participating and even denying one's own personal

pleasure for the moment." Finally we are told that the new "ethic of commitment" might be a commitment to "people, institutions, objects, beliefs, ideas, places, nature, projects, experiences, callings," etc. A lot of the utopian verbiage floating around Yankelovich's "ethic of commitment" has the ring of "more belief," even though he places it in the context of a fundamental shift in social values predicted to take place sometime in the future. Such speculation is grist for the cynic's mill. "Sharing, giving, sacrificing, participating, 'Give me a break!'" Nonetheless Yankelovich has a realistic side as well. "Sooner or later the psychology of affluence will be forced to yield to a social ethic better suited to the new economic realities. Before it does, we can expect a period of intense political conflict," he informs us.[8] Yanekelovich may be right on this point, but we are yet to see any evidence of a radical correction to the left. As long as America remains locked in the anesthetizing grip of consumerism, significant political change seems unlikely. Meanwhile, the growing epidemic of cynicism in America cripples political reform and scorns attempts at meaningful action. In the end, Yankelovich's prediction of future "intense political unrest" could be optimistic, for real change might only arrive on the heels of violent social unrest.

Words like "community," "commitment," and "connectedness" are a part of many belief-oriented cures for cynicism. Historian Zachary Karabell takes a shot at predicting the future in his *A Visionary America*. Karabell predicts that in the "next stage" of American history, the nation will turn to "connectedness." He envisions an era in which the national goals will be "to increase intimacy; enhance self-awareness; carve out time and space for friendships, family, and community; establish ecological harmony; create demographic balance; and promote greater understanding of the non-material aspects of human existence. The utopian vision of connectedness" he continues, "will dream of a society in which people focus on their own emotional growth with the same fervor, sophistication and intensity that they now focus of enhancing the New Economy." Again, this is a thoughtful prediction, but one that appears to be wrapped in the language of some sort of New Age belief. With words like "intimacy" and "friendships," we can almost hear the cynic snicker and perhaps mumble something about the Bobsey Twins. Still, Karabell is realistic. The final solution to America's restless utopian wanderings, he tells us, is "a society that learns from its past, takes stock of its present, and takes time to consider the future." According to Karabell, this is "profoundly improbable," for it "rests on an optimistic appraisal of American society." That is to say, it rests on the restoration of the American Dream.[9]

The belief remedy even appears in the most analytical of assessments. Take for example the ideas of Phillip Brown and Hugh Lauder in *Capitalism and Social Progress*. These scholars propose a total re-thinking of the relationship between the individual and society. "Market Individualism," they tell us, is no longer viable in the modern economy; what is needed is "Collective Intelligence," a revolutionary new economic and social substance that insists ". . . all are capable rather than just a few." At the heart of collective intelligence is the notion that "the pooling of intelligence, through the creation of social structures which enhance the capacity for intelligent action, offers the best prospect of prosperity, democracy, and social harmony in the context of post industrial development. If the twentieth century is dominated by the spirit of competition, the twenty-first century must begin in an attempt to create a spirit of co-operation." Again the cynic licks his chops— Yeah! We've really got to pull together on this one. He's heard it all before. It'll never work. It does not matter how right-thinking the calls for cooperation, community, and belief might be, cynicism is as immune to logic, common sense, and clear thinking as it is to emotionalism and blind faith. As with all of these remedies, Brown and Lauder's collective intelligence can only grow in an atmosphere of belief. "The pooling of intelligence is impossible to achieve in societies characterized by market individualism, by low trust and by social polarization," they tell us. "Unless people have a stake in society and feel economically secure and believe they have a future, the capacity for exercising collective intelligence is compromised." Which is to say that until materialism, cynicism, and social inequality are defeated and a realistic national dream restored, their solution will not work.[10]

Many of the solutions proposed by modern American intellectuals today involve the creation of a new social "ethic," "covenant," or "compact," a national redefining of the relationship between the individual and society. This may indeed be the solution, but it is a tall order, and few offer much help as to how to achieve such a sweeping social revolution, even though many feel that such a revolution is inevitable. In *Democracy on Trial*, Jean Bethke Elshtain addresses sweeping social change realistically, ". . . it will be difficult," she writes, ". . . unless Americans . . . can once again be shown that they are all in it together; unless democratic citizens remember that being a citizen is a civic identity, not primarily a private sinecure; unless government can find a way to respond to peoples' deepest concerns, a new democratic social covenant has precious little chance of taking hold."[11]

The examples are seemingly endless because it is hard to pose a cure for cynicism without a call for belief. But no matter how pragmatic and down-to-earth, they all have that naïve utopian ring of cooperation, intimacy, and community. What is more, many are couched in lofty, academic rhetoric that makes them easy marks for the sarcasm of the cynic's earthy arrows. As William Chaloupka points out, "Most of the responses a believer can formulate in the face of mounting cynicism only make matters worse." And there are still more problems with belief. "The persistent difficulty for belief," Chaloupka warns, "is that it can be manipulated. Belief can be feigned or tricked. . . ."[12]

At the bottom of the issue of belief lies the simple fact that without addressing the basic issues causing our disappointment, more belief will only breed more cynicism. The stronger the belief, the more heartbreaking the disappointment, and the more staunch the resulting cynicism. It is no coincidence that the same forces that create cynicism, a condition of too little belief, can also create fundamentalism, a condition of too much belief. No, more belief alone is not the answer.

With the gleaming sword of belief thus at least temporarily ensheathed, we must resume our frontal assault on cynicism in America seemingly unarmed. To find the chink in its armor, we must begin by confronting the problem areas that we identified in our initial assessment at the beginning of this chapter. These are three: cynicism itself, the so-called Modern Condition, and the present American Dream.

Confronting Cynicism

Confronting cynicism takes patience and persistence. It is a task for realists. As Arnett and Arneson wisely advise, "We must take the world on its own terms, with endurance, tenacity, and hope, aware of the ever potential face of danger." Despite the danger, this "head on" approach is far better than giving up, far superior to giving in to cynicism or to embracing some utopian blind faith that things will somehow work out for the best. But there is risk involved. Jedediah Purdy might be addressing the American cynic when he speaks of irony in *For Common Things,* "There is something fearful in this irony [cynicism]. It is a fearful betrayal, disappointment, and humiliation, and a suspicion that believing, hoping, or caring too much will open us to these." In short, it senses a world of risk. Still, if we are willing to take the risk, there is much to gain. We just might even get our dreams back.[13]

All great fighters understand the value of knowing their enemy. To combat cynicism we must understand the mind of the cynic, join his camp, affirm those insights he may have that are important. Again, Purdy's ironist offers insight into the wisdom of the cynic, "The successful ironist [cynic] holds himself at enough distance from his surroundings to . . . avoid involving himself in treachery, depravity or worthlessness. . . . The ironist is the eternal enemy of hypocrites and fanatics, people falsely confident in their own goodness or absurdly certain that their ideas are the only true ones. . . ."[14] We must understand that in some cases "cynical evaluations and actions are . . . appropriate,"[15] but that while the survival mentality of cynicism "may offer ingredients for short term individual success, it presents a long term hazard for society."[16]

Most of all we must remember this: there *is* a cure for cynicism—a cure that has been obvious since the first ranting of the Cynics of ancient Greece. Remember, we said that Diogenes and the early Greek Cynics "distrusted words and demanded action." This is the answer: we must act. Arnett and Arneson put it concisely, "Confidence and trust replace cynicism only where you consistently deliver on your promises."[17] Put another way, the cure for cynicism is success. If so, we must be careful how we dream. We must dream prudent dreams that have a reasonable chance to achieve modest, demonstrable realizations. Most important, we must be very careful how we define success.

This is our advantage. We can act and we can dream. Today's cynic can act only symbolically. His dreams are dead, and he has given up. He can only defend—this is his weakness. He is not willing to take risks. If he does act in any way other than to bar action or to criticize, he ceases to be a cynic and rejoins us in the world of action and hope.

Diogenes himself gave us the solution. Sloterdijk gives us the method. "Only a radical nakedness and bringing things out in the open can free us from the compulsion for mistrustful interpretations. Wanting to get to the naked truth is one motive for sensuousness, which wants to tear through the veil of conventions, lies, and abstractions and discretions in order to get to the bottom of things." Then he adds provocatively, "A mixture of cynicism, sexism, 'matter-of-factness' and psychologism constitutes the mood of the superstructure in the West, a twilight mood, good for owls and philosophy."[18] We must end this twilight in which cynicism thrives.

As Jedediah Purdy reminds us, today our own speech avoids sincerity, avoids the truth, ". . . it is difficult today to speak earnestly about personal matters; to speak earnestly about public issues seems perverse: not only naïve, but wrongly or confusedly motivated." But we must speak earnestly and bravely.

To do so, like Diogenes, we must employ a lamp; not the cynic's lamp of sarcasm and mockery, but a lamp to expose and illuminate the naked truth. We must find, embrace, and become Diogenes' honest man.

Confronting the Modern Condition

The first step in exposing the "naked truth" is to come to grips with our present situation. That is to say, we must face up to and confront the so-called Modern Condition. Here the term the Modern Condition is used simply in its most widely understood sense: Western man's inability to deal with the sweeping changes wrought by industrialism, urbanization, the creation of a mass society, and the loss of individualism, which have together combined to create widespread feelings of powerlessness, isolation, moral ambiguity, alienation, dependency, melancholy, and uncertainty. In his *Critique of Cynical Reason,* Sloterdijk informs us that the Modern Condition predisposes us to cynicism, while in *Cynicism and Postmodernity,* Timothy Bewes insists that cynicism is a result of the "ratification of the Postmodern Condition."[19] Whatever the case, for our purposes let us just say that cynicism is a natural human reaction to the disappointments inherent in the Modern Condition.

To confront the Modern Condition in a bold and courageous way, we must begin by acknowledging the fact that it is here to stay. There is little we can do to change things in this regard. What we can change is the way we deal with it. The problems of the Modern Condition are not so much the rapid changes that have taken place in society, but our own inability to cope with these changes. Our values, our institutions, our culture, and our very dreams themselves have become antiquated and false. They are in dire need of radical modification, yet we cling to them like children to so many worn out rag dolls. We have not only lost the ability to act, we have forgotten how to dream.

If we have the courage to act, our dreams can again save us. As Arthur Schlesinger Jr. so eloquently puts it, "Free men accept the limitations of the human intellect and the infirmity of the human spirit. The distinctive human triumph . . . lies in the capacity to understand the frailty of human striving and to strive nonetheless." But, for what are we to strive? We must build an up-to-date, realistic American Dream rooted in the "naked truth." In the words of Jedediah Purdy, we must invite "a realignment of our moral imagination to what is at hand." Only then can we end the cycle of disappointment, end cynicism in America, and dovetail our hopes with the realities of the Modern Condition. "Sometimes just having a dream is the key to a better life."[20]

Confronting the American Dream

Confronting cynicism in America and the harsh realities of the Modern Condition requires courage, but unless we also confront the problems associated with the American Dream, our efforts to end cynicism in America and to learn to live with the Modern Condition will be to no avail. And, as stated in the Preface, this book contends that cynicism in America is the result of a recent shift in the American Dream.

Few will deny the obvious problems that cynicism and the Modern Condition pose for contemporary American society, and most non-cynics would support action to address these problems. A large part of the solution is recognizing and correctly defining the problem and then honestly facing up to the situation. But when it comes to confronting the American Dream, things are not so straightforward. Cynicism and the Modern Condition are things that have happened to us as a nation. They are historical forces against which we can join together to defend ourselves. However, the American Dream is a part of our national soul, and as such, criticizing it, to say nothing of altering it, requires an act of self-mutilation. Still, the American Dream, as it now exists, contains elements of a cancer that must be removed. The insights needed for this kind of "autosurgery" are perhaps beyond the wisdom of most Americans. Meddling with the American Dream may appear to many to be nothing less than blasphemy.

Fortunately, not all of the American Dream is infected. The central core of the dream is still as valid and as healthy as ever, but much has been added that is malignant and false. We must closely examine the current Dream and remove only those elements that do not line up with the reality in which we presently find ourselves.

Rebuilding the Foundation of the American Dream. First, we must begin to rebuild the old foundation of the American Dream that has been ruinously eroded by the forces of industrialization, urbanization, and mass society. We must replace the old acquisitive American individualism

with a new modern kind of individualism and exchange the old Puritan work ethic for a new collective social ethic. This is a tall order indeed. It requires nothing short of redefining the individual's relationship to society as a whole. This kind of social upheaval takes time and cannot be mandated overnight. Still, it can be urged along.

Individualism came to the New World from Europe, from the Renaissance and from the Enlightenment. It was then mingled with a crude, resilient frontier ethic to form something uniquely American. For Americans, individualism became the great amalgam of their national identity, a crude mixture of liberty and democracy and *laissez faire,* a melting pot of political, social, and economic being unlike anything the world had seen before. It was rooted in the natural law of Locke and Jefferson, and it insisted that, when left alone, unfettered by government, each man acting for his own best interest would result in the maximum good for all.

For the first immigrants, the Old World had been hard and the American frontier perhaps at first even harder. So it is not surprising that with the first breezes of capitalistic prosperity, Americans molded their powerful new individualism into an assertive, grasping, material impulse. Americans had had enough of the hardships and deprivation of Europe and of the American frontier. By the late nineteenth century, the acquisitive side of American individualism and the material side of the American Dream were in ascendance, and more new immigrants were pouring in seeking El Dorado.

It is important to remember that the early settlers who brought European individualism to America and modified it on the frontier were immigrants. Later more immigrants built upon this foundation. For the immigrants that today flock to our shores, the American Dream is real. Material? Yes. But also idealistic, as before. For many new American immigrants, the Dreams of liberty and democracy, of family and work, still resound with undeniable authenticity. These immigrants are not corrupted by expectations of entitlements, nor are they arrogant, and their material aspirations are modest by our standards.

We were all once immigrants; we must all become immigrants again. Leaving our old world behind, we must seek new beginnings in a new modern world; we must dream better dreams. There is another, older side to the American Dream and another side to American individualism. As Alexis de Tocqueville noted in *Democracy in America* way back in the 1830s, there is the grasping kind of individualism, which leads to tyranny; but there is also what he called "individualism properly understood," which first sees to the common good of society and leads to successful democracy. This is the only kind of individualism that will fit the modern circumstance. If we can find it, then we can build a modern cooperative social ethic aimed at individual self-realization, not only through work as before, but also through interpersonal commonality. None of this is intended to imply that the material side of the American Dream must be discarded, only that it must be moderated and brought back into balance with the idealistic side of the Dream.

The American playground of the frontier is gone, and the new material toys no longer satisfy—it is time for America to grow up. How fitting that the road map for the future beyond the frontier should come from the one who best defined its importance for us all, Frederick Jackson Turner. "But if there is disillusionment and shock as we come to realize the changes," Turner wrote, "there is challenge and inspiration in them too. In place of the old frontiers of wilderness, there are new frontiers fruitful for the needs of the race; there are frontiers of better social domains yet explored."[21]

It will take generations to replace the foundations of the American Dream, to build a new individualism and a new social ethic. While that work is underway, we can address the corruptions of the various parts of the Dream itself.

Renovating the Idealistic Side of the American Dream.

The original core of the American Dream has fared better than the rest. Most Americans still seem to cherish personal liberty and the Bill of Rights with fervor. Some have come to take these promises for granted, and some feel that the myriad encroachments of modern big government have eroded our freedoms. Still, a lively dialogue remains, and in the most fundamental sense, we are still free to rise, although it must quickly be added that some of us are a great deal freer to rise than others.

Sadly, the American Dream of democracy has not held up as well. This is partly because we have not seen to the universal and equitable distribution of hope and partly because we have come to mistrust politics and government. This is tragic, because if action and truth are indeed the remedies for cynicism, then these remedies must be brought to bear in the arena of politics. As Chaloupka concludes, "In sum, the solution is politics—lively, contentious, serious, smart public struggle over issues that matter."[22] The American Dream of democracy is a dream of politics. It is a dream that can only be realized if we act politically to restore the hard, naked truth to the rhetoric of politicians through changes in campaign regulations, the media, and ourselves. We must loudly reject hollow patriotic rhetoric no matter how articulate and moving. We must reward only the truth, no matter how raw and unpleasant it may be. Only then can we end the cycle of mistrust and regain our lost political power.

Modifying the Material Side of the American Dream.

There is no reason why we should not enjoy the fruits of our economic success, and there is nothing wrong with the material side of the American Dream except our obsessive, exclusive fixation upon it. It has been a driving force in our progress since the beginning. We must learn to deal with the gifts of the Dream, and curb the inflated value we have come to place on material wealth. Over the decades, materialism has come to stand in for our lost individualism. It is a hollow substitute for the new civic-minded individualism we require. At the root of the problem is the fact that, for most Americans, material wealth has become the measure of success. To the extent that we continue to define success in terms of material possessions and financial power, the American Dream will continue to disappoint. Real success is a matter of accomplishment, not status symbols. Accomplishment might be economic in nature, but it also might be civic, spiritual, communal, familial, or interpersonal. Success is a matter of self-fulfillment, not material enrichment.

At the bottom of the problem with America's current false notion of success lies the American Dream of progress. Of all of the dreams in the American experience so far, this is by far the most fallacious, the most audacious, the most ignorant, and the most fickle. It is a dream that is guaranteed to disappoint. The self-aggrandizing idea that American progress will continue on an uninterrupted upward curve, that each generation will be better off than the one before it, is an impossible utopian dream that would be laughable if it were not so damaging. It is pure self-manufactured, nationalistic propaganda, and the sooner we stop clinging to this national lie, stop teaching it to our children, stop believing it despite all evidence to the contrary, the sooner we can realistically redefine success and get on with our modern national journey. Again, the solution is to face up to the naked truth.

Demolishing Arrogant Dreams. One way to destroy the ruinous American Dream of progress and rein in the material side of the American Dream is to discard all the ignorant and arrogant lesser American dreams upon which the Dream of progress has been built. These are the self-centered, nationalistic dreams of American superiority—dreams of know-how, world power, ingenuity, business acumen, entrepreneurship—supercilious dreams of moral, cultural, governmental, scientific, and economic pre-eminence. Not really dreams at all, they are rather over-blown national myths, based on a numbing national ignorance and a widespread xenophobia born of misguided nationalism. These egotistical notions, inconsistent with present world realities, defeat us in all of our efforts abroad. Out of them grows an unlovely fundamentalism that seeks to spread American ideas to every corner of the planet. In our stubborn refusal to "accept the pluralistic destiny of mankind,"[23] we are misguidedly attempting to make the world over in our own image. It is no wonder that the American Dream of progress is destined to disappoint, based as it is on a blind, nationalistic egotism that is inconsistent with the true state of both domestic and world affairs.

Adjusting Other American Dreams.

There are a few more minor adjustments needed to restore the American Dream to its former preeminence as the guiding hope and aspiration of a nation of dreamers.

The American Dream of education is generally intact and workable, although it is still lacking with regard to equality of access. One could argue over finance, methods, consistency, and so on, but healthy dialogues seem to be continuing. If there is a problem with the American Dream of education, it is that it is tainted by its association with the American Dream of progress, which insists that part of the measure of our progress is that each generation be better educated than the one that went before. What is more, America's materialism has further infected the Dream of education with the belief that a college education is a necessary rung on the ladder to success. Here again, it is the hollow, materialistic definition of success that causes the stain. There is no reason to believe that one cannot be a valuable and self-fulfilled member of society without a college education, unless, of course, one's value and fulfillment are measured solely in material terms.

Lastly, let's consider the Standardized American Dream: a house in the suburbs, two cars, and the ever-expanding list of attendant "necessary" products and services. As we have said, there is nothing wrong with the material side of the American Dream—nothing, that is, beyond its disproportionate preeminence over the idealistic side. If one finds satisfaction in its codified material trinkets, then one should seek the realization of that Dream. The problem with the Standardized American Dream is that it has been artificially inseminated into our culture. It is not a real dream at all. Our needs for the luxuries and commodities listed in the Standardized Dream grow from cultural urges that are planted not by real-life experience, but by the media and by advertising. The implantation of these mass needs is a cynical manipulation, a blatant untruth that confounds any efforts to end cynicism by insisting on the "naked truth."

Confronting the Current American Dream. Lastly

we must come to grips with the current American Dream, the obsessive preoccupation with celebrity and the vague yearnings for some kind of windfall good luck. It is a dream characterized by fixations on get-rich-quick schemes, on a growing litigiousness, and on the "money-for-nothing" rewards of sport, pop music, media, and popular culture. This is certainly a twisted kind of romanticism, a flight of fancy away from reality and into a world all its own. The passing of the old individualism is clearly reflected in such fantasies as more and more Americans look to pop idols and stars in an impossible search for vicarious individuality. Likewise, the end of the old work ethic is reflected in mindless dreams of gratuitous reward and windfall wealth.

Sadly, the construction of a successful new, modern social ethic to replace the loss of individualism and the work ethic is the only real cure for the shallowness of the current American Dream. As we have noted, this will probably be a long time coming. In the meanwhile, we must work to repair the American dream, to make it more realistic and relevant and rid it of corruptions. If we can do this, if we can begin to deliver on our promises, then perhaps the fantasy dreams of celebrity and gratuitous wealth will begin to have diminished appeal.

In repairing the American Dream, the most important thing to remember is that it must remain a dream. Something potentially real, not a fantasy; something to aspire to, not something promised; a realistic hope, not an expectation; an attainable goal, not an entitlement. If we can purge the Dream of romantic fantasies, nationalistic delusions, unrealistic expectations, egoisms, and arrogance; if we can make its constituent parts realistic and accessible within the context of the new mass society, we can then come to grips with the Modern Condition and slowly end cynicism in America. The Modern Condition is about hopelessness. The New American Dream is about hope. No cynic dares to hope.

A Question of Balance

As we have seen, the history of America can be told as a saga of the ongoing struggle between the idealistic side of the American Dream and the materialistic side of the American Dream. It is significant to note that in past periods of frustration and uncertainty we always modified the machinery used to realize the dream, but did not really modify the core Dream itself. This modified machinery has taken many forms. Examples of mechanisms aimed at strengthening the idealistic side of the Dream are Jacksonian democracy, progressivism, and the welfare state; examples of mechanisms aimed at strengthening the material side of the Dream include *laissez faire* capitalism and the new market economy. The central core of the American Dream has remained more or less the same: that we remain free to rise.

Still, over time, there have been additions to and manipulations of the Dream, many resulting in over-promise. And the material side of the American Dream has overpowered the idealistic side, resulting in a widespread shallowness of vision. Again, the result has been disappointment and cynicism.

It is now time for alterations to the Dream itself. We need a new American Dream, not more machinery designed to manipulate and prop up the old one. The core of the Dream is sound, but we must cut away the various corruptions in order to bring the two sides of the American Dream back into equilibrium. The suggestions detailed above are designed to do just this: to curb the voracious appetites of the materialistic Dream, to cut away arrogance and egoism and to lift the idealistic Dream back into a position from which it can again temper the material Dream and thus sustain balance. It is all a question of balance. When in proper alignment, the realization of the material side of the dream provides a prosperous, secure atmosphere for the dreams of the ideal side to blossom; and the realization of the ideal side of the Dream provides an atmosphere for the Dreams of the material side to continue their support. To attain this balance, some of the old dreams must be sacrificed for new and better dreams.

We have a difficult task ahead. It will require realism, and dreamers are seldom realistic. They often dream beyond their grasp. If we fail to make our new dreams reachable, we risk a downward spiral of cynicism. "There is a danger in all visions," as Karabell reminds us. "They are potentially totalitarian in that they reduce reality to a simple set of values. Not usually known for humility, visionaries often reject nuance and try to silence dissent."[24] The creation of a new American Dream will require the nuance of balance. A new American Dream will take decades to fashion, and cynicism will not disappear overnight. In the meantime, we must face the naked truth, and walk the line between reality and hope. As Arnett and Arneson put it, ". . . we need to walk between the extremes of ignoring the reality and power of cynicism in everyday life and languishing in its daily prevalence, attempting to avoid entrapment in routine cynicism by embracing contrasting sides of the human spirit. It is possible to embrace hope about what human beings can accomplish together and simultaneously not be blind to the significant evil humans have done and are capable of doing."[25] Or as Christopher Lasch puts it, ". . . we need to recover a more vigorous hope . . . without denying life's tragic character."[26] It is all a question of balance. Until a new American Dream is completed and a new social ethic becomes a reality, a delicate balance must be achieved between the two different methods employed by modern man to protect himself from the uncertainty that surrounds him. Cynicism and hope, caution and possibility, they just might be self-correcting companions.[27] Together they might provide just the balance needed to build a new American Dream.

Notes

Preface

1. Parrington, *Main Currents,* 3: xxiii.

2. Walt Kelly, *Pogo.*

Chapter 1

1. Purdy, *For Common Things,* 95, 212, xi, 203.

2. Purdy, *For Common Things,* 6, 16.

3. Purdy, *For Common Things,* xiv-xv, 42.

4. Purdy, *For Common Things*, xi, xxii.

Chapter 2

1. Chaloupka, *Everybody Knows,* 71.

2. Dudley, *History of Cynicism*, xi.

3. Sloterdijk, *Critique of Cynical Reason*, 102.

4. Branham and Goulet-Caze, *The Cynics*, 1, 22, 5; Chaloupka, *Everybody Knows*, 4; Branham and Goulet-Caze, *The Cynics*, 22.

5. Branham and Goulet-Caze, *The Cynics*, 5, 4–5; Sloterdijk, *Critique of Cynical Reason*, 101; Chaloupka, *Everybody Knows*, 3.

6. Branham and Goulet-Caze, *The Cynics*, 4–5.

7. Dudley, *History of Cynicism*, 5.

8. Branham and Goulet-Caze, *The Cynics*, 16, 21, 18–20.

9. *American Heritage Dictionary 2000*; Branham and Goulet-Caze, *The Cynics*, 25; Sloterdijk, *Critique of Cynical Reason*, 4; *Oxford English Dictionary,* 2nd ed.

10. *New Oxford American Dictionary; American Heritage Dictionary*, 2000; *New Oxford American Dictionary.*

11. Sloterdijk, *Critique of Cynical Reason*, 217–8, xxix, 304.

12. Chaloupka, *Everybody Knows*, 46.

13. Arnett and Arneson, *Dialogic Civility*, 13; Sloterdijk, *Critique of Cynical Reason*, 6; Chaloupka, *Everybody Knows*, 12; Sloterdijk,

Critique of Cynical Reason, 30.

14. Arnett and Arneson, *Dialogic Civility*, 25.

15. Sloterdijk, *Critique of Cynical Reason*, 29.

16. Goldfarb, *Cynical Society*, 1, 13, 22.

17. Chaloupka, *Everybody Knows*, xv.

18. Arnett and Arneson, *Dialogic Civility*, 13, 17, 19.

19. Goldfarb, *Cynical Society*, 2–3, 16.

20. Daniel Kinney, "Heirs of the Dog;" in Branham and Goulet-Caze, *The Cynics*, 294; Chaloupka, *Everybody Knows*, 12.

21. Sloterdijk, *Critique of Cynical Reason*, 4.

22. Chaloupka, *Everybody Knows*, 45.

23. Sloterdijk, *Critique of Cynical Reason*, 3, 7, 4, 5.

24. Bewes, *Cynicism and Postmodernity*, 1.

25. Walter Rathenau, *On the Critique of the Times*, 67–9.

26. Sloterdijk, *Critique of Cynical Reason*, 309.

27. Eliot, *Complete Poems and Plays*, 271.

28. Kanter and Mirvis, *Cynical Americans,* 87; Sloterdijk, *Critique of Cynical Reason*, 6, 22, 5.

29. *Oxford English Dictionary*, 2nd ed.

30. Chaloupka, *Everybody Knows*, xiv.

31. Jost, "Negative Illusions," 303.

32. Augoustinos and Walker, *Social Cognition*, 9.

33. Jost, "Negative Illusions," 303.

34. *Random House Webster's College Dictionary*, 1999; Andreas Huyssen, foreword to Sloterdijk, *Critique of Cynical Reason*, xiii.

35. Sloterdijk, *Critique of Cynical Reason*, 5; Niehues-Probsting, "Modern Reception of Cynicism," 333.

36. Sloterdijk, *Critique of Cynical Reason*, 4.

Chapter 3

1. John Wise, *Vindication of the Government of the New England Churches*, quoted in Parrington, *Main Currents*, 1:123; William Dunlap, 1790; Carpenter, *American Literature and the Dream*, 6; James Truslow Adams in *The Epic of America*, quoted in Cullen, *American Dream*, 4; Blum, *Promise of America*, 191; Karabell, *Visionary Nation*, 5–7.

2. Clark, *Immigrants and the American Dream*, 4; J. Hochschild, *Fac-*

ing Up to the American Dream, 14.

3. Campbell, *Hero with A Thousand Faces.*

4. Marx, *Machine in the Garden*, 3.

5. F. Scott Fitzgerald, *The Great Gatsby.*

6. Turner, *The Frontier in American History*, 38.

7. Parrington, *Main Currents*, 1:145; Turner, *The Frontier in American History.*

8. Marx, *Machine in the Garden*, 26–7.

9. Dudley, *History of Cynicism*, 212.

10. Yankelovich "New Rules," 43; Clark, *Immigrants and the American Dream*, 4.

11. Goldfarb, *Cynical Society*, 18.

12. de Tocqueville, *Democracy in America.*

13. Potter, "Quest for the National Character," 72.

14. Gill, *Posterity Lost*, xvi.

15. Lasch, *Culture of Narcissim*, 52–3; Scharhorst, *Horatio Alger, Jr.*, 9.

16. Clark, *Immigrants and the American Dream*, 2.

17. Adams, John, Notes for *A Dissertation on the Canon and Feudal Law* (1765).

18. Blum, *Promise of America*, 152–3.

19. Blum, *Promise of America*, 151.

20. Newman, *Declining Fortunes*, ix.

21. Marx, *Machine in the Garden*, 131.

22. Marshall, *Celebrity and Power*, 242; Cowen, *What Price Fame?*, 8; Horkheimer and Adorno, "The Culture Industry: Enlightenment as Mass Deception," in *Dialectic of Enlightenment*, 123-71; Marshall, *Celebrity and Power*, 9, 10; Lowenthal, "Triumph of Mass Idols," 109–40; Marcuse, *One Dimensional Man.* Quoted material is Marshall discussing Lowenthal's and Marcuse's work.

23. Whyte, *Organization Man*, 22-3.

24. Eisenberger, *Blue Monday,* 58.

25. Lerner, "Big Technology," 85.

26. Lasch, *Culture of Narcissism.*

Chapter 4

1. Parrington, *Main Currents,* 1:x.

2. Bronowski and Mazlish, *Western Intellectual Tradition*, 62.

3. Bronowski and Mazlish, *Western Intellectual Tradition*, 81; Martin Luther, *Treatise on Christian Liberty*.

4. Bronowski and Mazlish, *Western Intellectual Tradition,* 90; Parrington, *Main Currents*, 1:12.

5. Fiske, *Beginnings of New England,* 9.

6. Ergang, *Europe,* 390.

7. Fiske, *Beginnings of New England,* 45.

8. Bronowski and Mazlish, *Western Intellectual Tradition,* 174.

9. Morison, *Oxford History of the American People,* 74.

10. Morison, *Oxford History of the American People,* 61.

11. Parrington, *Main Currents*, 1:52; Fiske *Beginnings of New England*, 64.

12. Parrington, *Main Currents*, 1:47-8.

13. Walker, *Thomas Hooker*, 125.

14. Roger Williams, *Works*, 3:214.

15. Turner, *The Frontier in American History*, 30, 38, 65.

16. Morison, *Oxford History of the American People*, 52.

17. Karabell, *Visionary Nation*.

18. Parrington, *Main Currents*, 1:135, 133.

19. Parrington, *Main Currents*, 1:33.

20. de Crèvecoeur, *Land of Promise*, 55.

21. Bronowski and Mazlish, *Western Intellectual Tradition*, 202, 216.

22. Bronowski and Mazlish, *Western Intellectual Tradition*, 216, 263.

23. John Wise, *Vindication of the Government of the New England Churches*.

24. Ergang, *Europe*, 571.

25. Parrington, *Main Currents*, 1:135.

26. John Locke, *Two Treatises on Government*, 44.

27. Karabell, *Visionary Nation*, 32; Morison, *Oxford History of the American People*, 151, 180.

28. Parrington, *Main Currents*, 1:184; Samuel Adams, *Writings*, 3:244; Parrington, *Main Currents*, 1:189.

29. Parrington, *Main Currents*, 1:192; John Adams, "A Letter to Mr. Niles, 14 January 1818."

30. Karabell, *Visionary Nation*, 39.

31. Morison, *Oxford History of the American People*, 721.

32. Karabell, *Visionary Nation*, 36.

33. Morison, *Oxford History of the American People*, 236, 194.

34. Parrington, *Main Currents*, 1:194.

35. Parrington, *Main Currents*, 1:194.

36. Morison, *Oxford History of the American People*, 271.

37. Parrington, *Main Currents*, 1:282.

38. Parrington, *Main Currents*, 1:286.

39. Parrington, *Main Currents*, 1:301; Alexander Hamilton in a letter to James Duane, September 3, 1780; Alexander Hamilton, quoted in Parrington, *Main Currents*, 1:305.

40. Crowe, *American Thought and Society*, 42.

41. Parrington, *Main Currents*, 1:304.

42. Parrington, *Main Currents*, 1:306.

43. Eliot, *Debates*, 422.

44. Parrington, *Main Currents*, 1:328.

45. John Adams, *Works*, 4:408.

46. John Adams, *Works*, 6:484; quoted in Parrington, *Main Currents*, 1:321.

47. Parrington, *Main Currents*, 1:322–3.

48. Amos Singletary, quoted in Parrington, *Main Currents*, 1:287-8.

49. Parrington, *Main Currents*, 1:328.

Chapter 5

1. Parrington, *Main Currents,* 1:402.

2. Randolph.

3. Ames.

4. Morison, *Oxford History of the American People*, 368.

5. Karabell, *Visionary Nation,* 53.

6. Schlesinger Jr., *Age of Jackson,* 18.

7. Parrington, *Main Currents,* 2: 257.

8. Schlesinger Jr., *Age of Jackson,* 310.

9. Jefferson, "Notes on Virginia," *Writings*, 2 :230.

10. Bronowski and Mazlish, *Western Intellectual Tradition,* 335.

11. Morison and Commager, *Growth of the American Republic,* 1:510.

12. Boyer, *Enduring Vision,* 297.

13. Schlesinger Jr., *Age of Jackson,* 387.

14. Schlesinger Jr., *Age of Jackson,* 319.

15. Bronowski and Mazlish, *Western Intellectual Tradition,* 387.

16. Ergang, *Europe,* 575.

17. Schlesinger Jr., *Age of Jackson,* 315.

18. Schlesinger Jr., *Age of Jackson,* 314.

19. Sedgewick, *Public and Private Economy,* 2:19.

20. Bronowski and Mazlish, *Western Intellectual Tradition,* 348-9.

21. Adam Smith, *The Wealth of Nations,* 1:2.

22. James Fenimore Cooper, *The American Democrat,* 161.

23. Schlesinger Jr., *Age of Jackson,* 336.

24. Schlesinger Jr., *Age of Jackson,* 30.

25. Schlesinger Jr., *Age of Jackson,* 307, 313.

26. Schlesinger Jr., *Age of Jackson,* 313.

27. de Tocqueville, *Democracy in America,.*

28. Parrington, *Main Currents,* 3:xxviii.

29. Carpenter, *American Literature and the Dream,* 9.

30. W. W. Rostov, *Stages of Economic Growth,* 7.

31. Parrington, *Main Currents,* 2:371.

32. Parrington, *Main Currents,* 2:378.

33. Ralph Waldo Emerson, *Journals,* 242.

34. Thomas Paine, quoted in Henry David Thoreau, *Civil Disobe-
    dience,* quoted in Parrington, *Main Currents,* 2:403.

35. Schlesinger Jr., *Age of Jackson,* 387.

36. Parrington, *Main Currents,* 2:437.

37. Carpenter , *American Literature and the Dream,* 8.

38. Marx, *Machine in the Garden,* 27.

39. Carpenter, *American Literature and the Dream,* 8.

40. Carpenter, *American Literature and the Dream,* 8.

41. Marx, *Machine in the Garden,* 181.

42. Parrington, *Main Currents,* 2:57.

43. Karabell, *Visionary Nation,* 58.

44. Parrington, *Main Currents,* 2:465.

Chapter 6

1. Parrington, *Main Currents,* 3:102.

2. Walt Whitman, "Democratic Vistas," *Prose Works,* 254–55.

3. Morison, *Oxford History of the American People,* 316.

4. Karabell, *Visionary Nation,* 72.

5. Parrington, *Main Currents,* 3:12.

6. Turner, *The Frontier in American History,* 1, 145.

7. Turner, *The Frontier in American History,* 259.

8. Parrington, *Main Currents,* 3:284.

9. Mark Twain, *Puddin' Head Wilson, A Tale,* 1894.

10. Parrington, *Main Currents,* 3:91.

11. Twain, *Notebook,* 1898.

12. Twain, *Pudd'nhead Wilson's New Calendar,* 1897.

13. Parrington, *Main Currents,* 3:100.

14. Munford, *Brown Decades,* 5.

15. Fleming, "Social Darwinism," 125.

16. Lerner, "Triumph of *Laissez faire*," 151.

17. Lerner, "Triumph of *Laissez faire*," 165.

18. Parrington, *Main Currents,* 3:190, 192.

19. Turner, *The Frontier in American History,* 307.

20. Parrington, *Main Currents,* 3:404.

21. Parrington, *Main Currents,* 3:266.

22. McGerr, *Fierce Discontent,* 29.

23. Morison, *Oxford History of the American People,* 822.

24. Karabell, *Visionary Nation,* 87.

25. Karabell, *Visionary Nation,* 88.

26. Commager, *American Mind,* 406–7.

27. Kronenberger, "H. L. Menken," 102.

28. Kronenberger, "H. L. Menken," 103.

29. Parrington, *Main Currents,* 3:366.

30. Commager, *American Mind,* 265.

Chapter 7

1. Lerner, "Big Technology," 85.

2. Lerner, "Big Technology," 85.

3. Morison, *Oxford History of the American People,* 892.

4. Karabell, *Visionary Nation,* 95.

5. Schlesinger Jr., "Sources of the New Deal," 389.

6. Chaloupka, *Everybody Knows,* 32.

7. Karabell, *Visionary Nation,* 97.

8. McGerr, *Fierce Discontent,* 29.

9. Magdoff and Sweezy, *End of Prosperity,* 128.

10. Patterson, *Grand Expectations,* viii.

11. Jones, *Great Expectations,* 38–9.

12. Patterson, *Grand Expectations,* 65–6.

13. Chaloupka, *Everybody Knows,* 33.

14. George Kennan, *Memoirs,* 228.

15. Reisman, *Lonely Crowd*.

16. Whyte, *Organization Man*, 4–7.

17. Patterson, *Grand Expectations*, 342.

18. Lyndon B. Johnson, Speech, University of Michigan, May 1964.

19. Karabell, *Visionary Nation*, 101.

20. Lyndon B. Johnson; quoted in Sandel, *Democracy's Discontent*, 283.

21. Chaloupka, *Everybody Knows*, 63.

22. Karabell, *Visionary Nation*, 104.

23. Emerson, Ralph Waldo, *Self Reliance*.

Chapter 8

1. Karabell, *Visionary Nation*, 4-5.

2. Whyte, *Organization Man*, 22-3.

3. Kanter and Mirvis, *Cynical Americans*, 6.

4. Wrightsman, "Measurement of Philosophies," 743-51; Rosenberg, *Occupations and Values*; Kanter and Mirvis, *Cynical Americans*, 287-300.

5. Howe, "Mass Society," 194-6.

6. Howe, "Mass Society," 194-6.

7. Sloterdijk, *Critique of Cynical Reason*, 112.

8. Morison, *Oxford History of the American People*, 271.

9. Berthoff, *Republic of the Dispossessed*, 2.

10. Kanter and Mirvis, *Cynical Americans*, 5.

11. Parrington, *Main Currents*, 1:277.

12. Toffler, *Future Shock*.

13. Arnett and Arneson, *Dialogic Civility*, 19.

14. Eisenberger, *Blue Monday*, 28, 58; Jones, *Great Expectations*, 283.

15. Goldfarb, *Cynical Society*, 13.

16. Kanter and Mirvis, *Cynical Americans*, 5.

17. Kanter and Mirvis, *Cynical Americans*, 6.

18. Daniel Yankelovich, *The Yankelovich Monitor*, 1978.

19. *The Harris Survey* (1966; September 13–25, 1973; January 3–7, 1986).

20. Kanter and Mirvis, *Cynical Americans*, 5.

21. Schlesinger Jr., "One Against the Many," 531, 532.

22. Schlesinger Jr., "One Against the Many," 532.

23. John Kenneth Galbraith.

24. Himmelstein, *Television Myth,* 19–20, 24.

25. Sloterdijk, *Critique of Cynical Reason,* 307.

26. Maynard, *Looking Back,* 3–4.

27. Purdy, *For Common Things,* 13 and xii.

28. Sloterdijk, *Critique of Cynical Reason,* 307, 308.

29. Kanter and Mirvis, *Cynical Americans,* 14.

Chapter 9

1. Kanter and Mirvis, *Cynical Americans,* 87, 3.

2. Kronenberger, "H. L. Menken," 103.

3. Howe, "Mass Society," 206.

4. Arnett and Arneson, *Dialogic Civility,* 11.

5. Goldfarb, *Cynical Society,* 22.

6. Chaloupka, *Everybody Knows,* 82.

7. Daniel Boorstin, *The Image,* 75.

8. Chaloupka, *Everybody Knows,* 16.

Chapter 10

1. Karabell, *Visionary Nation,* 198, 213, 197.

2. Cullen, *American Dream,* 10; Arnett and Arneson, *Dialogic Civility,* 25.

3. Purdy, *For Common Things,* 185, 186, 207, xxi.

4. Purdy, *For Common Things,* xvi, xviii–xix, xviii, xx, xxi, xxii.

5. Purdy, *For Common Things,* xviii-xix, xviii, xx, xxi, xxii.

6. Purdy, *For Common Things,* 194, 196.

7. Chaloupka, *Everybody Knows,* 15.

8. Yankelovich, *New Rules,* ix, 213, 250, 125, 250, 213.

9. Karabell, *Visionary Nation,* 208, 214.

10. Brown and Lauder, *Capitalism and Social Progress,* 3, 10.

11. Jean Bethke Elshtain, *Democracy on Trial,* 30–31.

12. Chaloupka, *Everybody Knows,* 19.

13. Arnett and Arneson, *Dialogic Civility,* 26; Purdy, *For Common Things,* xii.

14. Purdy, *For Common Things,* 212.

15. Lasch, *Culture of Narcissim,* 84.

16. Arnett and Arneson, *Dialogic Civility,* 12.

17. Arnett and Arneson, *Dialogic Civility,* 21.

18. Sloterdijk, *Critique of Cynical Reason,* xxxviii.

19. Bewes, *Cynicism and Postmodernity,* 7.
20. Schlesinger Jr. "One Against the Many," 537; Purdy, *For Common Things,* 202; Cullen, *American Dream,* 7.
21. Turner, *The Frontier in American History,* 300.
22. Chaloupka, *Everybody Knows,* 223.
23. Schlesinger Jr., "One Against the Many," 537.
24. Karabell, *Visionary Nation,* 139.
25. Arnett and Arneson, *Dialogic Civility,* 23.
26. Lasch, *True and Only Heaven,* 530.
27. Arnett and Arneson, *Dialogic Civility,* 25.

Bibliography

Adams, James Turlson. *The Epic of America* (1931). Reprint, Garden City, NY: Blue Ribbon Books, 1944. Quoted in Cullen, *American Dream*, 4.

Adams, John. Notes for *A Dissertation on the Canon and Feudal Law* (1765). In Butterfield, L. H., ed. *Diary and Autobiography of John Adams*. Cambridge, MA: Harvard University Press, 1961. Quoted in Parrington, *Main Currents*, 1:184.

———. A letter to Mr. Niles, January 14, 1818. Quoted in Parrington, *Main Currents*, 1:184.

———. *The Works of John Adams: Second President of the United States . . .*, 10 vols. ed. Charles Francais Adams. Boston: Charles C. Little and James Brown, 1850–56. Quoted in Parrington, *Main Currents*, 1:305.

Adams, Samuel. *The Writings of Samuel Adams*, 4 vols., ed. H. A. Cushing. New York: P. G. Putman's Sons, 1904–08. Quoted in Parrington, *Main Currents*, 1:251.

Ames, Fisher. Quoted in Morison, *Oxford History of the American People*, 368.

Arnett, Ronald, and Pat Arneson. *Dialogic Civility in a Cynical Age: Community, Hope and Interpersonal Relationships*. Albany, NY: State University Press of New York, 1999.

Augoustinos, Martha, and Iain Walker., ed. *Social Cognition: an Integrated Introduction*. London: SAGE Publications, 1995.

Beard, Charles A., and Mary R. Beard. *The Rise of American Civilization*. New York: MacMillin and Company, 1930.

Berthoff, Roland. *Republic of the Dispossessed: The Exceptional European Consensus in America*. Columbia and London: University of Missouri Press, 1977.

Bewes, Timothy. *Cynicism and Postmodernity*. New York: Verso, 1997.

Blum, John Morton. *The Promise of America: An Historical Inquiry*.

Boston: Houghton and Mifflin Company, 1966.

Boorstin, Daniel. *The Image: A Guide to Pseudo-Events in America.* New York: Antheneum, 1961. Quoted in Lasch, *Culture of Narcissism*, 75.

Boyer, Paul S., et al. *The Enduring Vision: A History of the American People.* Lexington, MA: D.C. Heath and Company, 1993.

Branham, R. Bracht, and Marie-Odile Goulet-Caze, ed. *The Cynics: The Cynic Movement in Antiquity and Its Legacy.* Berkley: University of California Press, 1996.

Bronowski, J., and Bruce Mazlish. *The Western Intellectual Tradition: From Leonardo to Hagel.* New York: Harper Brothers, 1960. Reprint, New York: Harper & Row, Publishers, Incorporated, 1962.

Brown, Phillip, and Hugh Lauder. *Capitalism and Social Progress: The Future of Society in a Global Economy.* New York: Palgrave, 2001.

Bush, Clive. *The American Dream of Reason: American Consciousness and Cultural Achievement from Independence to the Civil War.* New York: St. Martin's Press, 1977.

Campbell, Joseph. *The Hero with A Thousand Faces.* Princeton: Princeton University Press, 1968.

Carpenter, Fredrick I. *American Literature and the Dream.* New York: Philosophical Library, 1955.

Chaloupka, William. *Everybody Knows: Cynicism in America.* Minneapolis: University of Minnesota Press, 1999.

Clark, William A. V. *Immigrants and the American Dream: Remaking the Middle Class.* New York: The Guilford Press, 2003.

Commager, Henry Steele. *The American Mind: An Interpretation of American Thought and Character Since 1880.* New Haven: Yale University Press, 1950.

Cooper, James Fenimore. *The American Democrat.* Quoted in Schlesinger, Jr., *Age of Jackson,* 339.

Cowen, Tyler, *What Price Fame?* Cambridge, MA: Harvard University Press, 2000.

Crowe, Charles Robert. *A Documented History of American Thought and Society.* Boston: Allyn and Bacon, 1965.

Cullen, Jim. *The American Dream: A Short History of an Idea That Shaped a Nation.* Oxford: Oxford Press, 2003.

de Crèvecoeur, M. G. St Jean. *Letters from an American Farmer.* New

York: Fox, Duffield, and Company, 1904.

Delbanco, Andrew. *The Real American Dream: A Meditation on Hope.* Cambridge, MA: Harvard University Press, 2001.

de Tocqueville, Alexis. *Democracy in America.* Quoted in Delbanco, *Real American Dream*, 67.

de Tocqueville, Alexis. *Democracy in America.* 2 vols. New York: Henry G. Langley, 1845.

Dudley, Donald R. *A History of Cynicism from Diogenes to the 6th Century A.D.* New York: Gordon Press, 1974.

Dunlap, William. *The Father*, 1790. Quoted in Beard and Beard, *Rise of American Civilization*, 469-70.

Eisenberger, Robert. *Blue Monday: The Loss of the Work Ethic in America.* New York: Paragon House, 1989.

Eliot, Jonathan. *Debates in the Several State Constitutions on the Adoption of the Federal Constitution . . .*, 4 vols. Washington; 5 vols. Philadelphia, 1906. Quoted in Parrington, *Main Currents*, 1:305.

Eliot, T. S. "The Family Reunion." In *The Complete Poems and Plays of T. S. Eliot, 1909–1950.* New York: Harcourt, Brace & World, Inc., 1952.

Elshtain, Jean Bethke, *Democracy on Trial.* New York: Basic Book, 1995.

Emerson, Ralph Waldo. *Journals of Ralph Waldo Emerson, with Annotations*, 10 vols., ed. Edward Waldo Emerson and Waldo Emerson Forbes. Boston, Houghton Miflin, 1909–14. Quoted in Parrington, *Main Currents,* 3:391.

Ergang, Robert. *Europe from the Renaissance to Waterloo.* Boston: D. C. Heath and Company, 1954.

Fiske, John. *The Beginnings of New England or the Puritan Theocracy in Its Relations to Civil and Religious Liberty.* New York: Houghton, Mifflin and Company, 1898.

Fitzgerald, F. Scott. *The Great Gatsby.* New York: Charles Scribner's and Sons, 1925. Quoted in Marx, *Machine in the Garden*, 360.

Fleming, Donald. "Social Darwinism." In *Paths of American Thought,* ed. Arthur M. Schlesinger Jr. and Morton White (Boston: Houghton, Mifflin and Company, 1963), 125.

Furnham, Adrian. *The Protestant Work Ethic: The Psychology of Work-related Beliefs and Behaviors.* London: Routledge, 1990.

Galbraith, John Kenneth. *The Affluent Society*. Boston: Houghton Miflin, 1976. Quoted in Schlesinger, Jr. and White, *Paths of American Thought*, 532

Gill, Richard T. *Posterity Lost: Progress, Ideology, and the Decline of the American Family*. Lanham: Rowman & Littlefield Publishers, Inc., 1997.

Goldfarb, Jeffrey C. *The Cynical Society: The Culture of Politics and the Politics of Culture*. Chicago: The University of Chicago Press, 1991.

Greenberg, Stanley B. *Middle Class Dreams: The Politics of Power of the New American Majority*. New York: Times Books, 1995.

Hamilton, Alexander. Quoted in Parrington. *Main Currents,* 1:305, 307.

Himmelstein, Hal. *Television Myth and the American Mind*. 2nd ed. Westport: Praeger Publishers, 1994.

Hochschild, Jennifer. *Facing Up to the American Dream: Race, Class, and the Soul of the Nation*. Princeton, NJ: Princeton University Press, 1996. Quoted in Cullen, *American Dream*, 6.

Horkhiemer, Max, and Thodor Adorno. "The Culture Industry: Enlightenment as Mass Deception," in *The Dialectic of Enlightenment*. New York: Continuum, 1972. Cited in Marshall, *Celebrity and Power,* 9.

Howe, Irving. "Mass Society and Post Modern Fiction." In *The Dilemma of Organizational Society,* ed. Hendrick Ruitenbeek. New York: E. P. Hutton & Co., 1963.

Jefferson, Thomas. *The Writings of Thomas Jefferson*, 20 vols. Memorial Edition. Washington, D.C.: The Thomas Jefferson Memorial Association of the United States, Lipscomb, 1904–05. Quoted in Schlesinger Jr., *Age of Jackson*, 310.

Johnson, Lyndon B. Quoted in Sandel, *Democracy's Discontent*, 283; quoted in Karabell, *Visionary Nation,* 101.

Jones, Landon Y. *Great Expectations: America and the Baby Boom Generation*. New York: Coward, McCann & Geoghegan, 1980.

Jost, J. T. "Negative Illusions, Conceptual Clarification and Psychological Evidence Concerning False Consciousness." In *Social Cognition, an Integrated Introduction,* ed. Martha Augoustinos and Iain Walker. London: SAGE Publications, 1995.

Kanter, Donald L., and Philip H. Mirvis. *The Cynical Americans: Living and Working in an Age of Discontent and Disillusion.* San Francisco: Josey Bass Publishers, 1989.

Karabell, Zachary. *A Visionary Nation: Four Centuries of American Dreams and What Lies Ahead.* New York: Harper and Collins, 2001.

Kennan, George. *Memoirs, 1950–1963.* Boston: Little, Brown, 1972. Quoted in Patterson, *Grand Expectations,* 203–4.

Kinney, Daniel, "Heirs of the Dog: Cynic Selfhood in Medieval and Renaissance Culture." In *The Cynics: The Cynic Movement in Antiquity and its Legacy,* ed. Branham and Goulet-Caze. Berkley: University of California Press, 1996.

Kronenberger, Louis. "H. L. Menken." In *Critical Essays on H. L. Mencken,* ed. Douglas C. Stenerson. Boston: G. K. Hall & Co. 1987.

Lasch, Christopher. *The Culture of Narcissism: American Life in an Age of Diminishing Expectations.* New York: W. W. Norton & Company, Inc., 1978. Also quoted in Furnham, *Protestant Work Ethic,* 227.

―――. *The True and Only Heaven: Progress and Its Critics.* New York: W. W. Norton & Company, Inc., 1991.

Lerner, Max. "Big Technology and Neutral Technicians." In *The Dilemma of Organizational Society,* ed. Hendrik M. Ruitenbeek. New York: E. P. Hutton & Co., 1963.

―――. "The Triumph of Laissez-Faire." In *Paths of American Thought,* ed. by Arthur M. Schlesinger Jr. and Morton White. Boston: Houghton, Mifflin and Company, 1963.

Locke, John. *Two Treatises on Government,* 9 vols., ed. Thomas I. Cook. New York: Hafner Publishing Company, 1947. Quoted in Bronowski and Mazlish, *Western Intellectual Tradition,* 211.

Longman, Phillip. *The Return to Thrift: How the Coming Collapse of the Middle Class Welfare State Will Reawaken Values in America.* New York: The Free Press, 1996.

Loving, Jerome. *Emerson, Whitman and the American Muse.* Chapel Hill and London: The University of North Carolina Press, 1982.

Lowenthal, Leo. "The Triumph of Mass Idols." In *Literature,*

Popular Culture and Society. 1944. Palo Alto, CA: Pacific, 1961. Cited in Marshall, *Celebrity and Power,* 10.

Luther, Martin, *Treatise on Christian Liberty.* Quoted in Parrington, *Main Currents,* 1:12.

Magdoff, Harry, and Paul M. Sweezy. *The End of Prosperity: The American Economy in the 1970s.* London: Monthly Review Press, 1977.

Marcuse, Herbert. *The One Dimensional Man: Studies in the Ideologies of Advanced Industrial Society.* Boston: Beacon, 1992. Cited in Marshall, *Celebrity and Power,* 10.

Marshall, David. *Celebrity and Power: Fame in Contemporary Culture.* Minneapolis: University of Minnesota Press, 1997.

Marx, Leo. *The Machine in the Garden: Technology and the Pastoral Ideal in America.* London: Oxford University Press, 1964.

Maynard, Joyce. *Looking Back: A Chronicle of Growing Up in the Sixties.* New York: Doubleday, 1973.

McGerr, Michael A. *Fierce Discontent: The Rise and Fall of the Progressive Movement in America, 1870-1920.* New York: Free Press, 2003.

Morison, Samuel Eliot. *The Oxford History of the American People.* New York: Oxford University Press, 1965.

Morison, Samuel Eliot, and Henry Steele Commager. *Growth of the American Republic.* 2 vols. New York: Oxford University Press, 1942.

Munford, Lewis. *The Brown Decades: A Study in the Arts in America, 1865-1895.* New York: Harcourt, Brace and Company, 1931.

Newman, Katherine S. *Declining Fortunes: The Withering of the American Dream.* New York: Basic Books, 1993.

Niehues-Probsting, Heinrich. "The Modern Reception of Cynicism, Diogenes in the Enlightenment." In *The Cynics: The Cynic Movement in Antiquity and Its Legacy,* ed. Branham, R. Bracht and Marie-Odile Goulet-Caze. Berkley: University of California Press, 1996.

The Oxford History of the American People, s.v. "Randolph, John."

Parrington, Vernon L. *Main Currents in American Thought.* 3 vols. 1927. New York: Harcourt, Brace and World, Inc.; Norman, OK: University of Oklahoma Press, 1930.

Patterson, James T. *Grand Expectations: The United States, 1945–1974*. New York: Oxford University Press. 1996.

Potter, David M. *People of Plenty: Economic Abundance and American Character*. Chicago: University of Chicago Press, 1954.

———. "The Quest for the National Character." In *Individualism and Conformity in the American Character,* ed. Richard L. Rapson. Lexington, MA: D.C. Heath and Company, 1967.

Purdy, Jedediah. *For Common Things: Irony, Trust and Commitment in America Today*. New York: Vintage Books, 2000.

Rapson, Richard L., ed., *Individualism and Conformity in the American Character*. Lexington, MA: D. C. Heath and Company, 1967.

Rathenau, Walter. *On the Critique of the Times*. Quoted in Sloterdijk, *Critique of Cynical Reason,* 437-38.

Reisman, David, et al. *The Lonely Crowd: A Study of the Changing American Character*. New Haven: Yale University Press, 1950.

Rosenberg, M. *Occupations and Values*. Glencoe, IL: Free Press, 1957.

Rostow, W. W. *The Stages of Economic Growth, A Non-Communist Manifesto*. Cambridge: Cambridge University Press, 1960. Quoted in Marx, *Machine in the Garden,* 26–7.

Ruitenbeek, Hendrik M., ed., *The Dilemma of Organizational Society*. New York: E. P. Hutton & Co., 1963.

Sandel, Michael. *Democracy's Discontent*, 283; quoted in Karabell, *Visionary America*, 101.

Scharhorst, Gary. *Horatio Alger, Jr.* Boston: Twayne Publishers, 1980.

Scharnhorst, Gary, and Jack Bales. *The Lost Life of Horatio Alger*. Bloomingdale, IN: Indiana University Press, 1985.

Schlesinger Jr., Arthur M. *The Age of Jackson*. Boston: Little, Brown and Company, 1954.

———. "The One Against the Many." In *Paths of American Thought*, ed. Arthur M. Schlesinger Jr., and Morton White. Boston: Houghton, Mifflin and Company, 1963.

———. "Sources of the New Deal." In *Paths of American Thought*, ed. Arthur M. Jr., and Morton White. Boston: Houghton, Mifflin and Company, 1963.

Sedgewick, Theodore. Quoted in Schlesinger Jr., *Age of Jackson,* 315.

Schlesinger Jr., Arthur M., and Morton White, ed., *Paths of American Thought.* Boston: Houghton, Mifflin and Company, 1963.

Sedgewick, Theodore. *Public and Private Economy.* New York: Harper and Brothers Publishers, 1836. Quoted in Schlesinger, Jr., *Age of Jackson*, 315.

Sloterdijk, Peter. *Critique of Cynical Reason.* Translated by Michael Eldred. Minneapolis: University of Minnesota Press, 1987.

Smith, Adam, *The Wealth of Nations.* Quoted in Schlesinger, *Age of Jackson,* 314.

Stenerson, Douglas C., ed. *Critical Essays on H. L. Mencken.* Boston: G. K. Hall & Co. 1987.

Toffler, Alvin. *Future Shock.* New York: Random House, 1970.

Twain, Mark. Quoted in Parrington, *Main Currents*, 3:91.

Turner, Frederick Jackson. *The Frontier in American History.* 1920. New York: Holt, Reinhart and Winston. Repr., Huntington, NY: Robert E. Kieger Publishing Co. Inc., 1976.

Walker, G. L. *Thomas Hooker, Preacher, Founder, Democrat.* New York: Dodd Mean and Company, 1891. Quoted in Parrington, *Main Currents,* 1:59.

Whitman, Walt. "Democratic Vistas." *The Complete Prose Works of Walt Whitman.* Boston; Small, Maynard and Company, 1898. Quoted in Parrington, *Main Currents,* 3:82.

Whyte, William H., Jr. *The Organization Man.* New York: Simon and Schuster, 1956.

Wilhite, Virgle Glenn. *Founders of American Economic Thought and Policy.* New York: Bookman Associates, 1958.

Williams, Roger. *The Works of Roger Williams,* 6 vols. Edited by members of the Narragansett Club Providence: Narragansett Club Publications, 1866–74. Quoted in Parrington, *Main Currents,* 3:24.

Winthrop, John. Quoted in Parrington, *Main Currents,* 1:59, 69.

Wise, John, *A Vindication of the Government of the New England Churches Drawn from Antiquity* . . . (1717). Boston, 1860. Quoted in Parrington *Main Currents,* 1:123.

Wrightsman, L. "Measurement of Philosophies and Human Nature." In *Psychological Reports.* No. 14, 1964.

Yankelovich, Daniel. "New Rules in American Life: Searching for Self-Fulfillment in a World Turned Upside Down,"

Psychology Today, April 1981.

————. *New Rules: Searching for Self-Fulfillment in a World Turned Upside Down.* New York: Random House, 1981.

————. *The Yankelovich Monitor.* Quoted in Kanter and Mirvis, *Cynical Americans,* 5.

Index

Index

About the Author

Wilber W. Caldwell is an independent writer and photographer living in the North Georgia mountains. In 1996, after a long career in the music industry, Mr. Caldwell began to indulge a variety of personal interests, including history, architecture, photography, food, and philosophy. His published works include *The Courthouse and the Depot: The Architecture of Hope in an Age of Despair,* a study of railroad expansion and its effect on public architecture in the rural South 1833–1910, published in 2001; and *Searching for the Dixie Barbecue: Journeys into the Southern Psyche*, a humorous insight into the mind of the rural South masquerading as food writing, published in 2005. *Cynicism and the Evolution of the American Dream* is his first long work of social criticism.